In Their Own Way

Also by Thomas Armstrong:

Creating Classroom Structure
The Radiant Child

IN THEIR OWN WAY

Discovering and Encouraging Your
Child's Personal Learning Style

Thomas Armstrong, Ph.D.

JEREMY P. TARCHER, INC.
Los Angeles
Distributed by St. Martin's Press
New York

For Leo

Library of Congress Cataloging in Publication Data

Armstrong, Thomas.
  In their own way.

  Bibliography.
  Includes index.
  1. Learning disabled children—Education—
United States. 2. Learning ability. I. Title.
LC4705.A76 1987   371.9   87–6445

ISBN 0–87477–446–2

Jeremy P. Tarcher, Inc.
9110 Sunset Blvd.
Los Angeles, CA 90069

Design by Robert Tinnon

Manufactured in the United States of America
10 9 8 7 6 5 4

Contents

Acknowledgments

For each book that I've written, there's been a "seed" I've been able to point to as the starting point of my labor of love, a shimmering wave of pregnant potential that gave witness to what was to come. For this book, it was a paper I wrote on December 12, 1973, for my first psychology class at the University of Massachusetts, in which I questioned the labels we give to children. My professor let me write the paper instead of doing a final exam, since I was scheduled to go overseas during finals week. So to Dr. Sheldon Cashdan, wherever you are, thank you for letting me fulfill the requirements of your class in my own way!

I was very lucky in my own school experience to have had several teachers who honored my intrapersonal style of learning. I want to especially thank Harold Washburn at the University of Massachusetts and George Hein, Cynthia Cole, Jill Hamilton, and Alice McKearney at Lesley College. These teachers had a deep respect for the integrity of children. Their seminars made a lasting impression on me that carried me through the years I spent floundering in the "worksheet wasteland" as a public and parochial school teacher. Thanks, too, to Elsom Eldridge and his brave but all too brief Educational Arts Association, which attempted to spearhead a grassroots campaign in our nation's schools to integrate the arts into the core curriculum.

My deep appreciation goes to many other individuals in my life who have inspired me in my work to follow my own way. These include Jack Canfield, Edith Sullwold, Lenore Lefer, and my parents, Dorothy and William Armstrong.

Several people deserve credit for providing resources, feedback, and support at various stages in the preparation of this manuscript including the late John Holt, Diane Divoky, Howard Gardner, Buff Bradley, Tony Prete, Robin Green, DeLee Lantz, Karen Kirzner, Alan Rinzler, Pacia Sallomi, John Arena, Suzanne Nus, Louise Bates Ames, Stanley Krippner, and Rowena Pattee.

My special thanks goes out to Brahmi Turner for all of her love and nurturance during the writing of *In Their Own Way*.

I cannot say enough good words about the people at Jeremy P. Tarcher, Inc.! It's been one of the great fortunes of my literary life to have had Janice Gallagher as my editor. Her challenging yet supportive attitude during our collaboration should be a model to other editors for how to get the best out of a writer. To publisher Jeremy Tarcher, who has brought the publishing world out of its own version of "the wasteland" into the clear light of day, thank you for believing in my message and helping me carry it to the nation. Thanks also to other Tarcher staffers for making me feel like family, including Laurie Held, Bud Sperry, Lynette Padwa, Amy Kastens, and Lori Horan.

Last, I must thank the hundreds of children who have flowed through my life during the past fifteen years—sometimes with the grace of a lazy country stream, and other times with the fury of a white water rapids! No matter how you've come to me—and no matter how you've left me—you've never been a label nor a percentile in my life. Your own wholeness always leaves me feeling just a little bit more complete.

Preface

*S*ix years ago I quit my job as a learning disabilities specialist. I had to. I no longer believed in learning disabilities. After teaching for several years in public and parochial special education classes in the United States and Canada, I realized I was going nowhere with a concept that labeled children from the outset as handicapped learners. I also began to see how this notion of learning disabilities was handicapping all of our children by placing the blame for a child's learning failure on mysterious neurological deficiencies in the brain instead of on much needed reforms in our systems of education.

After leaving my job I decided to write a book about the dangers of labeling children as disabled learners. In about two years time, I had a long, angry manuscript entitled *The Learning Disability Lie* that indicted the learning disability movement on several counts. However, something didn't feel quite right to me. After another year, it became apparent that I was still stuck, myself, in the negative consciousness I'd so roundly criticized in the field of learning disabilities. It was well and good to condemn something that was undermining a child's potential. But if the learning disability concept was so bad, what did I have to offer instead to explain why some children were not doing so well in school?

It was then that I turned to the concept of *learning differences* as an alternative to learning disabilities. I realized that the millions of children being referred to learning disabled classes weren't handicapped, but instead had unique learning styles that the schools didn't clearly understand. Furthermore, it seemed to me that the reason so many millions of additional children were underachieving, experiencing school phobias, or just plain bored in the classroom was because no one had recognized and used what they really had to offer in the learning place—their special talents and abilities. I began researching what had been discovered over the years about learning styles and found some amazing material that viewed children from the standpoint of growth rather than disability. I was particularly attracted to the ideas of Harvard psychologist Howard Gardner, who said that we all have seven different kinds of intelligence. It occurred to me that this material would be useful not only to parents who have kids in special education, but to all parents seeking to understand their children's personal learning styles. So, I essentially wrote a new book—the one you now have in your hands.

Chapter 1 of this book explains how the schools have failed to honor and develop special abilities and gifts in almost all of our nation's schoolchildren, even going so far as to send many of our most talented kids to classes for the learning disabled. Chapter 2 presents Gardner's theory of multiple intelligences—a perspective that promises to revolutionize the way we look at every child's learning potential. In this chapter, you'll learn how to identify your child's personal learning style. Chapters 3 and 4 examine current practices in testing and teaching children, exploring why these methods don't serve the children they're intended to help, and explaining what we need to do instead. Chapter 5 presents seven different ways you can help your child learn anything—including reading, math, spelling, and writing—based on Gardner's model.

The next eight chapters of the book really get into the heart of what learning is all about for any child. They explore eight different factors you need to know about in order to encourage your child's personal learning style, including putting the body back into learning, harnessing the imagination, addressing the emotions, creating quality relationships, nurturing positive expectations, developing a patient attitude as a parent, making use of all the senses, and improving the diet and other ecological factors.

An afterword explores the learner of the future, and how our so-called unmotivated and "learning handicapped" children instead may be the vanguard of a whole new way of processing information. The book concludes with a comprehensive collection of resources you can use to go even further in your efforts to help your child develop his or her own personal learning style. It includes the best books, periodicals, cassettes, and organizations I could find in the areas of child development, superlearning, parenting, the ecology of learning, childhood stress, human potential, neuropsychology, self-esteem, alternative learning styles, school options, and innovative approaches to the basic skills.

In Their Own Way will be useful to you whether you're the parent of a child in special education, the parent of an "underachiever" in the regular classroom, or the parent of a normally achieving—and possibly even high achieving— youngster who simply isn't getting much out of a public or private school education. If you're an adult with a unique learning style who had a hard time during your own school years, you too can find much in this book that will affirm and nourish your personal way of learning. Finally, if you're a teacher or mental health professional, you can use the concepts and techniques in this book to help the children you work with and, in addition, you can start to change the attitudes of your colleagues away from the deficiency consciousness so prevalent in modern day education and toward an appreciation of the giftedness in *all* learners.

It's clear to me after fifteen years of research and practice in the field of education that our schools are largely to blame for the failure and boredom that millions of children face as they trudge off unwillingly to their six-hour fate every weekday morning from September to June. Children categorized as learning disabled are the most visible casualties of this process, but they're not the only victims. In a sense, they're the tip of the iceberg. The system creates a stress that affects all children. In this book, I'm going to suggest basic improvements in the way that we help each and every child learn, so that one day terms like *learning disabilities, underachievement,* and *school phobia* will drop away from our vocabulary, and all of our children will be allowed to learn in their own way.

The Worksheet Wasteland: Neglecting Talents and Abilities in Our Nation's Schools

*B*illy loved to invent crazy machines. One of them caused water to run down a chute, moving ping-pong balls into sockets, in turn causing bells to ring and a miniature pig to spin around. This finally moved an alligator's head into which you could stick your pencil to be sharpened. Other machines did similarly creative and practical things. Yet in spite of these innovative projects, Billy was flunking out of school. He couldn't seem to do things the school's way. For example, when Billy's mother asked him to figure out the area of a room using the methods the school had taught him, Billy struggled. He tensed his body, erased frequently, and finally came up with a totally unrealistic answer.

Then Billy did it his way. "Billy shut his eyes and made little rhythmic movements with his head, as if he were listening to an inner song. After a while he jotted down something on the pad, closed his eyes for some more internal business, opened them, jotted something else down, and gave us the correct answer." Asked to describe the process, Billy responded, "Well, when I close my eyes to figure something out it's like a cross between music and architecture."

Susan was a first grader who read the encyclopedia for recreation. In reading class, she had to patiently submit to a curriculum that included books with titles like *ABC and Me* and *Little Pig*. Finally, the teacher asked the class to write a story about *Little Pig.* Susan wrote: "Little Pig, Little Pig. I'll tell you what you can do with Little Pig. You can take this book and . . ."

By the age of twelve, Chris was managing two profitable businesses at home and had a one-man art show at his elementary school. At five, Justin was giving talks on the solar system, creating elaborate Lego structures, and writing and illustrating his own original stories. Marc was an eleven-year-old Dungeons and Dragons expert, widely read on the subject. He also created animated movies. All three of these boys were labeled learning disabled by their school districts and forced to attend special remedial classes at their respective schools.

Each of the children described above is a unique learner whose gifts, talents, and abilities were ignored by the schools. They're not alone. Every year millions of children across the nation are being labeled as *learning disabled, dyslexic, hyperactive,* or *underachievers.* Millions more seem to be making satisfactory academic progress but are secretly dying inside because their true gifts and abilities are not being drawn out by the schools. Your child may be one of them. Here are some questions to ask yourself in order to discover if this is indeed the case.

- Does your child have some hobby, skill, interest, or ability that excites him at home? If so, is he getting a chance to use that talent or ability at school?
- When was the last time your child rushed home to tell you something important that he'd learned that day?
- Does your child like to hang around school at the end of the day, talking with the teacher, developing a project, practicing a skill, or does he rush off as soon as the bell rings?
- When you speak with the teacher about your child, what group of words does the teacher use most: *problems, needs, difficulties,* and *disabilities,* or *talents, accomplishments, interests,* and *abilities?*

- Does your child complain of stomachaches, headaches, and anxiety in the morning before going off to school, or does he talk at the breakfast table about all the exciting things he's going to be doing that day?
- Does your child bring home lots of textbooks, workbooks, and ditto sheets for homework, or does he instead have projects to work on that require real thought, creativity, and innovation?

The answers to these questions will give you a clue as to whether your child's school is nurturing his personal learning style. Chances are that you've just discovered that it isn't. The truth is that schooling for millions of children across the country is bland and boring. If your child sticks out one iota from the norm—in other words, if your child shows his true individual nature—then there is always the danger that he will be discriminated against or stuck with some sort of label and treated like a category instead of a real human being. Our schools have lost the ability to respond to individual differences. The purpose of this book is to help you regain that inner dignity for your children by discovering how they truly learn best and then helping them learn in their own way.

The Nation's Schools: A Worksheet Wasteland

Einstein once wrote, "It is nothing short of a miracle that the modern methods of instruction have not yet entirely strangled the holy curiosity of inquiry." His words ring especially true today in light of a recent study directed by John Goodlad, former dean of the School of Education at the University of California, Los Angeles. Goodlad's project, entitled "A Study in Schooling" and funded by over a dozen major foundations, was based on research in 1000 classrooms across the country and interviews with over 27,000 parents, teachers, and students. It represents the most wide-spread and detailed study of American classrooms ever undertaken.

The picture Goodlad leaves us with in his remarkable book *A Place Called School* is a wasteland of almost unbearably dull proportions. "Shared laughter, over enthusiasm, or angry outbursts were rarely observed. Less than 3 percent of classroom time was devoted to praise, abrasive comments, expressions of joy or humor, or somewhat unbridled outbursts such as 'wow' or 'great.' " Less than 1 percent of the day involved students in sharing opinions or openly reasoning about some problem or issue. Virtually all of the elementary school classrooms were dominated by the teachers, with students having next to no choice in how things were run. Nearly 70 percent of the classroom day was taken up with "talk," usually teachers lecturing to students. Goodlad reports that "a good deal of (students') time" was spent in elementary school classrooms just waiting for the teacher to hand out materials or tell them what to do. And over half of the children reported that many students did not know what was expected of them during much of the day.

The poverty reflected in these statistics is mirrored in students' attitudes toward their school experience. Goodlad noted that interest in *all* subjects declined from elementary school to senior high. For example, 56 percent of elementary school children reported that they enjoyed mathematics, while only 27 percent of senior high school students felt the same way. When students were asked "What is the one best thing about this school?" "my friends" and "sports activities" made up over half of the responses, while "classes" and "teachers" trailed far behind. When asked point blank "What have you learned?" one student replied, "To be honest, I haven't learned much. . . . I would like to, but all we do, or rather all she does, is talk and I get bored with the same routines everyday." Another student wrote: "Nothing we haven't learned before, and he's always writing referrals [for misbehavior]." Goodlad comments: "Films of relatively good frontal teaching (lecturing and questioning the whole class) clearly reveal how quickly many students turn their minds elsewhere or simply doze."

Reports from other sources confirm Goodlad's findings. Nationally, sales of duplicating paper are up, while sales of lined theme paper are down. A study conducted by Education Products Information Exchange noted that over half of the students already knew 80 percent of what was in their textbooks before they had even begun studying them. And a recent report by the Commission on Education and Public Policy of the National Academy of Education concluded that "workbook and skill sheet activities consume a large proportion of the time allocated to reading instruction in most American classrooms, despite the fact that there is little evidence that these activities are related to reading achievement." Clearly the schools are filling up our children's days with endless hours of busy-work.

Unfortunately, the proposed solution to what has been called "a rising tide of mediocrity" in America's schools turns out to be worse than the original problem. The most well-known of the commission reports of the 1980s, *A Nation at Risk,* recommends a longer school day and school year, "far more homework," more rigorous grading, more standardized tests, better textbooks, and adherence by all students to "the five new basics": English, math, science, social studies, and computer science—in other words, a more boring curriculum. Goodlad's study pointed out that elementary schools are already spending almost 80 percent of their instructional day in the basic skills, with art taking up only 7 percent of the school week, dance only 2 percent, and drama only 1 percent. The call for a more rigorous curriculum threatens to stifle individuality even more than is currently the case. According to Goodlad: "During the past 15 years . . . teachers have been exhorted to take account of and provide for student individuality in learning rates and styles. Our data suggest, however, that this is not something often or readily done. Students worked independently at all levels, but primarily on identical tasks, rather than on a variety of activities designed to accommodate their differences." One sees here the ominous vision of an assembly line classroom.

What happens to the learners in this worksheet wasteland? The truth is that most of them learn to comply and remain passive, even though they may outwardly appear to be very successful students. Goodlad points out: "The picture that emerges from the data is one of students increasingly conforming, not assuming an increasingly independent decision-making role in their own education." Other children, unable to go along with such stale fare as they're given daily in the classroom, begin slipping in their achievement but are able to keep up appearances to a greater or lesser degree. These are the underachievers that we keep hearing so much about. Lawrence Greene, in his book *Children Who Underachieve,* estimates that up to 50 percent of our nation's children are underachievers. Finally, there is a group of children totally unable to keep up with the charade, mostly because their own unique ways of learning clash so severely with the narrow way that the schools go about educating them. This group has earned an unjust name in recent years: learning disabled.

The Learning Disability Trap

On Saturday, April 6, 1963, a new disease was invented in Chicago, Illinois, that over the next twenty years would slowly begin to infect millions of schoolchildren nationwide. This was no simple virus or common bacteria. Hidden deep within the neurological system, it resisted detection by medical personnel, evaded clear diagnosis through testing, and had no discernible cure. The federal government would spend billions of dollars on this affliction over the next twenty years, and yet between 1977 and 1983 the number of sufferers would double.

It was on that Saturday in April that Samuel Kirk, then

a professor of special education at the University of Illinois, told a group of concerned parents about learning disabilities. He suggested that they use the term to describe "children who have disorders in development of language, speech, reading, and associated communication skills." They enthusiastically agreed and shortly thereafter established The Association for Children with Learning Disabilities.

Since that time, the learning disability (LD) movement has mushroomed, with the founding of many more organizations, the writing of hundreds of books and tens of thousands of articles. The popular media have made it a suitable subject for dramatic television shows and full-length feature films. More importantly, and devastatingly, millions of children have been labeled learning disabled, dyslexic, hyperactive, and a host of related terms, then sent to special programs to be treated for their "condition."

Yet, in spite of the impact of this term on the lives of children and adults around the country, the experts seem to be no closer to defining what it means, let alone to finding a cure for it. Bob Algozzine, a professor of special education at the University of Florida and contributing editor to *The Journal of Learning Disabilities,* wrote: "No one . . . has been able to demonstrate to me that a specific, distinctly unique group of behaviors differentiate LD children from many of their classmates. To build an empire on such a foundation is very dishonest." Douglas Friedrich and his colleagues at Central Michigan University studied 1600 children referred to specialists because of suspected learning problems, and in analyzing the ninety-four formulas that had been used to diagnose for learning disabilities, sadly noted: "It seems such a shame to subject persons to the life-long effects of the label 'learning disabled' when we really don't know what it is."

The LD movement, nevertheless, seems only to be growing stronger. Parents have been alerted to such warning signs of LD as reversals of letters and numbers, messy handwriting, poor coordination, problems telling time, confusion about right and left, and difficulty in reading. Psychologists continue to develop more intricate ways of testing for learning disabilities. Doctors experiment with new drug treatments—including lithium—for the "learning disabled" child.

Neglecting Learning Abilities

Nowhere in this litany of deficit, disability, and disease is there the recognition that these children may learn very well *in their own way.* This is because few researchers have bothered to look at how these youngsters learn best. Mary Poplin, former editor of *The Learning Disability Quarterly* (*LDQ*), comments:

> The horrifying truth is that in the four years I have been editor of *LDQ,* only one article has been submitted that sought to elaborate on the talents of the learning disabled. . . . Why do we not know if our students are talented in art, music, dance, athletics, mechanical repair, computer programming, or are creative in other nontraditional ways? . . . It is because, like regular educators, we care only about competence in its most traditional and bookish sense—reading, writing, spelling, science, social studies and math in basal texts and worksheets.

The one positive article that *was* submitted to her came from Dr. Sara Tarver and her colleagues at the University of Wisconsin's School of Education. They discovered that children labeled learning disabled scored higher than so-called normal children on tests of nonverbal creativity. Tarver also noticed that the so-called learning disabled children scored higher than "normals" in first grade on verbal scores but that their creativity in this area declined in the higher grades. She speculated that "one aspect of schooling which may contribute to the relative decline of learning disabled children's verbal creativity has to do with the negative reactions of others toward their uniqueness." In other words, these children are ridiculed by teachers and students for being creative, and they soon learn to keep a low profile, stifling their individuality in the process.

Other authorities affirm the inner richness of these youngsters. Harvard neurologist Norman Geschwind, until his death one of the leading figures in the field of learning disabilities, observed: "It is commonplace to hear parents of dyslexics say that they knew that a particular child would be dyslexic because like his dyslexic siblings . . . even at the age of three . . . he was showing unusual skill in drawing, or doing mechanical puzzles or building models." Jean Symmes, a psychologist with the National Institute of Child Health and Human Development, and Judith Rappaport, a psychiatrist at Georgetown University, studied a group of fifty-four children with learning problems and observed superior skills in three-dimensional spatial visualization. And Dorothy Bullock, an Arizona educator, found high levels of imagination in special education children referred for learning and emotional problems. In my own classes for the "learning handicapped," I had an amazing group of children: a boy who held the national freestyle swim record in his age group, a girl who was a model for a national department store chain, gifted artists and writers, a psychic child, expert storytellers, superior math students, and many other talented human beings.

And yet, when these children enter school, virtually all the focus of teachers and parents gets placed upon their "disability." It reminds me of the story about the animals who decided to create a school for climbing, flying, running, swimming, and digging. They couldn't agree on which subject was most important, so they said that all the students had to take the same curriculum.

The rabbit was an expert in running but almost drowned in swimming class. The experience shocked her so much that she never could run as well after that.

The eagle was a whiz at flying, of course, but when he

showed up for digging class, he was so inadequate to the task that he got assigned to a digging remediation program. It took up so much of his time that he soon forgot how to fly. And so forth with the other animals.

The animals no longer had the opportunity to shine in their areas of expertise because all were forced to do things that did not respect their individual nature. In much the same way, we're doing that with our children, neglecting their gifts and talents while at the same time forcing them to waste hours of time in boring and inappropriate remediation groups and special classes. Eagles are meant to fly!

Initiation into the Lie

I'd like to give you a picture of what goes on in the life of a child with a unique learning style, so that you can see how the schools methodically disengage people from their true potentials. Imagine an active and eager six-year-old girl brimming with excitement as she begins her first day of school. She's used to spending her days drawing, splashing around with friends at the local pond, playing ball on the neighborhood lot, building with blocks, and singing songs. As she enters the school on that momentous first day, she has expectations of being able to move about, explore things, sing, play, and interact with the other children. Instead, she finds herself in a world where she must sit in her seat for long periods of time, learn to decode long and complicated instructions from the teacher, and strain her eyes while looking at small squiggly numbers and letters in funny-smelling books.

When her disappointment and confusion become evident to the teacher, he refers her to a specialist for an evaluation. She is then subjected to a battery of tests that pick, poke, and prod at her inner world. The examiner dutifully records the many errors she makes. She easily catches onto the worry of her parents and teachers as they sit in conference talking about her problems.

Finally the "experts" diagnose her as having an official problem. Perhaps they call it *specific learning disability, dyslexia, hyperactivity, dysfunctional auditory sequential memory, attention deficit disorder, reading difficulty, math block,* or simply *underachievement.* The specialists prescribe a fancy treatment plan that is supposed to cure her of this dreaded condition. They place her in a special program—perhaps in a small room in a remote corridor of the school. Here, a teacher with special training "remediates" the learning problem using a wide range of esoteric methods and materials including walking on balance beams, behavior modification, and lots of worksheets. During recess, the child hears the other children talking about "the retards in Room 103."

Returning to the special class, she feels even more confused and restless. The teacher notices this, and during the next official meeting of the school team of professionals, they decide to keep her in the special program for at least another year. In this way, the child remains stuck in a cycle of learning failure, perhaps for the rest of her school days.

The above scenario may sound like a Kafkaesque nightmare, but it's an all too common occurrence in the public school system. I've not only seen this happen, I've participated in it. In spite of my best intentions and educational ideals, I found myself again and again being caught up in the workings of a system that has its own life and that seeks to turn children into defective merchandise sent back to the shop for repairs.

In the regular class, this child's peers may fare no better. Forced to abandon their own unique patterns of learning ability—their gifts, talents, and interests—they learn quickly to submit to a new way of learning that substitutes abstract symbols for living images and routine assignments for dynamic play. Their new life in this barren environment recalls what Kafka himself said about education in his own day: "Probably all education is but two things, first parrying of the ignorant children's impetuous assault on the truth, and second, gentle, imperceptible, step-by-step initiation of the humiliated children into the lie."

A New Focus: Honoring Each Child's Personal Learning Style

It's time for the schools, and parents as well, to start focusing their attention on the inner capabilities of each and every child. We've known for many years that human beings use only 5 percent of their potential—and I suspect that the percentage is actually much lower. If that's true, then in even the most brain damaged person there's a tremendous potentiality hidden within that is going un-tapped. John Lorber, a British pediatrician, studied one indi-vidual who, due to neurological illness, had virtually no brain. Instead of the normal 4.5-centimeter thickness of cerebral cortex, this young student had just a thin layer measuring a millimeter or so. In spite of this obvious shortcoming, he was measured as having an IQ of 126, was socially competent, and gained first-class honors in mathe-matics. Yet the schools persist in labeling hundreds of thousands of children with perfectly normal brains as "minimally brain damaged" or "neurologically handi-capped," when in fact teachers simply have not found a way of teaching them on their own terms, according to their own unique patterns of neurological functioning.

The part of the brain that thrives on worksheets and teacher lectures probably takes up less than 1 percent of the total available for learning. More likely, these stale methods of learning are actually what educator Leslie Hart refers to as "brain-antagonistic"—they shut down potentials rather than open them up. The 1,000 classrooms that John Good-lad's project surveyed are doing little beyond this: "Students were not very often called upon to build, draw, perform, role play, or make things." In other words, the children weren't given an opportunity to exercise the vast proportion of their brains devoted to new learning.

The children described at the beginning of this chapter were obviously very good at exploring uncharted regions of the brain—learning through music and architecture, words and feelings, business and film. Some people might consider them "gifted" and beyond the reach of the average schoolchild. But here they would be making the same mistake that is made by those who label children as "disabled learners." For by assigning the label of gifted to only a few selected individuals, we're shutting the door to millions more who possess untold inner riches. All children are gifted. Every child is a unique human being—a very special person. Every parent knows that.

Unfortunately, the schools prefer to send some kids to classes for learning disabilities, group others according to underachievement, and send a small group to programs for the gifted. They've even got a new category now for the "learning disabled/gifted" student. When will it ever end? It will end when parents decide to toss aside all of these labels and begin the task of understanding and nurturing their childrens' personal learning styles so that they can begin to learn in their own way. The next chapter presents a new model that will help you do this—Howard Gardner's theory of multiple intelligences.

CHAPTER 2

Seven Ways to Bloom: Discovering Your Child's Personal Learning Style

*P*eter can beat any challenger in a game of chess. Sally spends her free time listening to opera. Ed is a super-athlete. Frank entertains his peers with long-winded stories of adventure. Ann loves to draw and paint. June is always organizing a party or committee at school. David sits at home alone planning a business venture.

Although a typical IQ test might not show it, all of these children are highly intelligent. Each demonstrates a particular strength in one of seven different kinds of intelligence—logical-mathematical, musical, bodily-kinesthetic, linguistic, spatial, interpersonal, and intrapersonal—described by Harvard psychologist Howard Gardner in his prize-winning book *Frames of Mind*. This new model of intelligence has been called by Ernest Boyer of the Carnegie Foundation for the Advancement of Teaching the most exciting work currently being done in the field of learning. Gardner's theory of multiple intelligences provides a solid foundation upon which to identify and develop a broad spectrum of abilities within every child.

Gardner says that our society talks about only two or three of the seven types of intelligence when deciding who's smart in the culture. We look up to the highly linguistic person who reads and writes well, the logical thinker who reasons in clear and concise ways, and the rugged individualist with strong intrapersonal intelligence. Yet there are other equally valid forms of intelligence.

What about people who sing or dance well? Or those who can paint, draw, act, sculpt, invent or design? And what about individuals who are great leaders or have good intuition? These musical, bodily-kinesthetic, spatial, and interpersonal learners often get overlooked in discussions about superior intelligence.

This cultural neglect spills over into the classroom. Our schools prize mainly linguistic and logical-mathematical abilities. Children with talent in these areas will usually do well in school. But children with poor verbal or logical skills will often fail, even if they're highly talented in one or more of the other major intelligences. Gardner's model gives us a way of looking at the complete picture of a learner's potential so that these neglected abilities will be honored and developed as well.

Beyond the Right-Brained Learner

The theory of multiple intelligences certainly isn't the first model of human abilities ever created. For thousands of years, people have been trying to figure out better ways of describing and measuring intelligence levels —all the way from imbecile to genius. What makes Gardner's effort remarkable, however, is that he backs up his model with solid evidence from brain research, psychological testing, experiments with animals, developmental work with young children, descriptive accounts of exceptional ability, and cross-cultural studies.

Gardner's model is a vast improvement, for example, over the now outmoded right-brain/left-brain concept of neurological development. In the 1970s, psychologists and educators were telling us that the left hemisphere of the brain controlled logical, linear, and verbal abilities and the right hemisphere was responsible for creative, holistic, and spatial experiences. While there is still some truth to these observations, we now know that neurological organization is a much more convoluted affair (no pun intended). There's no such being as a "right-brained learner" unless it's someone who's had the left hemisphere of his brain removed! We use both hemispheres of our brain all of the time—as they interact with each other in complex ways and with other structures of the brain.

Gardner says that the seven kinds of intelligence are located in different parts of the brain. For most people, linguistic intelligence seems to be on the left side of the brain. Scientists have known for over a hundred years about Broca's area, a section of the left hemisphere that seriously affects speaking ability if damaged. Spatial and musical ability appear to be related to the right side of the brain. Logical-mathematical intelligence involves both sides—the left side remembers the symbols of math ($+$, $\times$, $=$, etc.) while the right side deals with the concepts. Bodily-kinesthetic intelligence takes in quite a few structures in the brain including the basal ganglia and the cerebellum. The personal intelligences are more complex. They appear to involve the prefrontal lobes of the brain—where damage can affect a person's ability to care for another person—while damage to other areas of the brain may result in a loss of interest in one's own self-care.

Even this neurological map is deceptively simple. There are many exceptions to these basic rules. While music ability may be located on the right side of the brain for most people, musically trained people tend to process melody on the left side of the brain as their ability to read music grows. The ability to speak is pretty much a task of the left hemisphere, yet if a person sings words, rather than simply says them, their ability to speak shifts over to the right side of the brain. This seems to be what happened to country-western singing star Mel Tillis, a severe stutterer, who met up with a "stranger" in his hotel room one night. He wanted to alert his sleeping roommate to the intruder—who later turned out to be his friend Johnny Paycheck who'd come in through the window in search of a lost key—but realized that he couldn't get the words out in time. So he began singing clearly and fluently, "We're being robbed." His musical right-brain was able to pick up the job that his stuttering left-brain couldn't handle under stress. In many other ways, different parts of the brain cooperate with each other, suggesting that the seven types of intelligence, while separate, spend a lot of time interacting with each other as well.

Culture Defines Who's "Disabled"

While our society favors linguistic, logical-mathematical, and intrapersonal abilities, other cultures put a very different emphasis on the seven varieties of intelligence. In the Anang society of Nigeria, for example, musical and bodily-kinesthetic intelligences are highly developed. By the age of five, the children of that society can sing hundreds of songs, play numerous percussion instruments, and perform dozens of complex dances. In Eskimo cultures, spatial intelligence is a major strength because Eskimos place a high survival value on noticing subtle differences in snow and ice surfaces. They don't want to be on the wrong side of a chunk of ice as it floats off into the sea! Sixty percent of the children in Eskimo cultures score as well as the top 10 percent of American children on tests of spatial aptitude. In certain South Seas island cultures, the ability to build and steer a canoe and navigate it by the stars—requiring superior bodily-kinesthetic and spatial intelligence—is very important. Finally, many non-Western cultures have highly evolved interpersonal intelligence where family or tribal bonds are so close that individual identity may simply not develop.

A highly literate person from our culture with superior linguistic or logical-mathematical intelligence might be at a real disadvantage in a South Seas island society. Without good spatial or bodily-kinesthetic skills, their "smarts" would be useless and they might even find themselves labeled "navigating disabled" learners.

I'm reminded of an ancient tale about a schoolteacher who hired an old man to take him across a river in a small boat. The scholar asked the old man whether the trip would be a difficult one. "I don't know nothing about it," replied the old man. The intellectual, noticing the boatman's poor grammar asked him, "Haven't you ever been to school?" "No," said the ancient mariner. "Well then, half your life has been wasted," retorted the schoolteacher. The old man didn't say anything but started the journey. When they got about halfway across, a big storm came up and the boat began to rock to and fro. The crusty sailor turned to the scholar and asked him if he knew how to swim. The teacher said he didn't, to which the old man replied, "In that case, your whole life is wasted, for we are sinking!"

This story suggests that an ability in one context is a real disability in another. On the other hand, a child labeled dyslexic, hyperactive, or learning disabled in our society might excel in another culture. The late Harvard neurologist Norman Geschwind once said:

> We happen to live in a society in which the child who has trouble learning to read is in difficulty. Yet we have all seen some dyslexic children who draw much better than controls . . . who have either superior visual-perception or visual-motor skills. My suspicion would be that in an illiterate society such a child would be in little difficulty and might in fact do better because of his superior visual-perception talents, while many of us who function well might do poorly in a society in which a quite different array of talents was needed to be successful. As the demands of society change, will we acquire a new group of "minimally brain-damaged"?

Gardner's model gives us a new way to understand the complete person—including both strengths and weaknesses—

without condemning anyone to "disabled learner" status for all time. More important, everyone has a chance to shine in some area of their lives. This makes Gardner's approach a wonderful tool for describing the abilities of children that the schools label or neglect in their rush to educate according to a narrow definition of competence.

Discovering Your Child's Personal Learning Style

Everyone has all seven kinds of intelligence in different proportions. Your child may be a great reader but a poor math student, a wonderful drawer but clumsy out on the playing field. Children can even show a wide range of strengths and weaknesses within one area of intelligence. Your child may write very well but have difficulty with spelling or handwriting, read poorly but be a superb story-teller, play an excellent game of basketball but stumble on the dance floor.

As you read through the descriptions of each type of intelligence that follow, resist the temptation to categorize your child into one of the seven intelligence groups. Your child is more complex than this. You should find your child described in several of the sections. Take what seems to apply to your child in these descriptions and add to this other observed strengths and weaknesses in all seven varieties of intelligence. Taken together, these constitute your child's personal learning style.

Linguistic Intelligence

Children gifted in linguistic ability have highly developed auditory skills and enjoy playing around with the sounds of language. They often think in words. They frequently have their head stuck in a book or are busy writing a story or poem. Even if they don't enjoy reading or writing, they may be gifted storytellers. They often love word games and may have a good memory for verse, lyrics, or trivia. They might want to be writers, secretaries, editors, social scientists, humanities teachers, or politicians. They learn best by verbalizing or hearing and seeing words. Linguistically gifted children:

- like to write;
- spin tall tales or tell jokes and stories;
- have a good memory for names, places, dates, or trivia;
- enjoy reading books in their spare time;
- spell words accurately and easily;
- appreciate nonsense rhymes and tongue twisters;
- like doing crossword puzzles or playing games such as Scrabble or Anagrams.

Logical-Mathematical Intelligence

Youngsters strong in this form of intelligence think conceptually. Before adolescence, these children explore patterns, categories, and relationships by actively manipulating the environment and experimenting with things in a controlled and orderly way. In their teen years, they're capable of highly abstract forms of logical thinking. Children gifted in this area are constantly questioning and wondering about natural events. These are the youngsters who love hanging around computers or chemistry sets, trying to figure out the answer to a difficult problem. They often love brain teasers, logical puzzles, and games—like chess—that require reasoning abilities. These children may want to grow up to be scientists, engineers, computer programmers, accountants, or perhaps even philosophers. Logical-mathematically talented children:

- compute arithmetic problems quickly in their head;
- enjoy using computers;
- ask questions like "Where does the universe end?" "What happens after we die?" and "When did time begin?";
- play chess, checkers, or other strategy games, and win;
- reason things out logically and clearly;
- devise experiments to test out things they don't understand;
- spend lots of time working on logic puzzles such as Rubik's cube.

Spatial Intelligence

These kids seem to know where everything is located in the house. They think in images and pictures. They're the ones who find things that have been lost or misplaced. If you should rearrange the interior of your home, these children will be highly sensitive to the change and react with joy or dismay. They often love to do mazes or jigsaw puzzles. They spend free time drawing, designing things, building with Lego blocks, or simply daydreaming. Many of them develop a fascination with machines and contraptions, sometimes coming up with inventions of their own. They might want to become architects, artists, mechanics, engineers, or city planners. Children strong in spatial intelligence:

- spend free time engaged in art activities;
- report clear visual images when thinking about something;
- easily read maps, charts, and diagrams;
- draw accurate representations of people or things;
- like it when you show movies, slides, or photographs;
- enjoy doing jigsaw puzzles or mazes;
- daydream a lot.

Musical Intelligence

Musically gifted kids often sing, hum, or whistle tunes quietly to themselves. Put on a piece of music and you can recognize these children by the way in which they immediately begin moving and singing along. They may already be playing musical instruments or singing in choirs. However, other musical children show this potential more through simple music appreciation. They will have strong opinions about the music you play on the radio or stereo. They will be the ones to lead a group sing on a family outing. They're also sensitive to nonverbal sounds in the environment—such as crickets chirping and distant bells ringing—and will hear things that others in the family have missed. Musically gifted children:

- play a musical instrument;
- remember melodies of songs;
- tell you when a musical note is off-key;
- say they need to have music on in order to study;
- collect records or tapes;
- sing songs to themselves;
- keep time rhythmically to music.

Bodily-Kinesthetic Intelligence

These children squirm at the breakfast table and are the first ones to be excused as they zoom out the door and head for the neighborhood playground. They process knowledge through bodily sensations. They get "gut feelings" about answers on tests at school. Some are primarily graced with athletic abilities or the skills of a dancer, actor, or mime—they are great at mimicking your best and worst qualities. Others are particularly gifted with excellent fine-motor coordination and can excel in typing, drawing, fixing things, sewing, crafts, and related activities. These children communicate very effectively through gestures and other forms of body language. Sometimes they can be labeled hyperactive at home and school if there aren't appropriate outlets for them. They need opportunities to learn by moving or acting things out. Children who excel in bodily–kinesthetic intelligence:

- do well in competitive sports;
- move, twitch, tap, or fidget while sitting in a chair;
- engage in physical activities such as swimming, biking, hiking, or skateboarding;
- need to touch people when they talk to them;
- enjoy scary amusement rides;
- demonstrate skill in a craft like woodworking, sewing, or carving;
- cleverly mimic other people's gestures, mannerisms, or behaviors.

Interpersonal Intelligence

These children understand people. They are frequently leaders among their peers in the neighborhood or in their class at school. They organize, communicate, and, at their worst, manipulate. They know what's going on with everybody in the neighborhood, who likes whom, who's feuding with whom, and who's going to fight whom after school. These youngsters excel in mediating conflict between peers because of their uncanny ability to pick up on other people's feelings and intentions. They might want to become counselors, business people, or community organizers. They learn best by relating and cooperating. Interpersonally gifted children:

- have a lot of friends;
- socialize a great deal at school or around the neighborhood;

- seem to be "street-smart";
- get involved in after-school group activities;
- serve as the "family mediator" when disputes arise;
- enjoy playing group games with other children;
- have a lot of empathy for the feelings of others.

Intrapersonal Intelligence

Like those who have interpersonal intelligence, intrapersonal children possess strong personalities. Yet many of them tend to shy away from group activities and prefer instead to bloom in isolation. They have a deep awareness of their inner feelings, dreams, and ideas. They may keep a diary or have ongoing projects and hobbies that are semisecretive in nature. There's a certain quality of inner wisdom, intuitive ability, or even a psychic nature that accompanies many of these children throughout their lives. This deep sense of self sets them apart and causes them to go off on their own toward some goal known only to themselves. They may want to become writers, small-business people running creative enterprises, or enter into religious work. Intrapersonally talented children:

- display a sense of independence or a strong will;
- react with strong opinions when controversial topics are being discussed;
- seem to live in their own private, inner world;
- like to be alone to pursue some personal interest, hobby, or project;
- seem to have a deep sense of self-confidence;
- march to the beat of a different drummer in their style of dress, their behavior, or their general attitude;
- motivate themselves to do well on independent study projects.

Gardner cautions against using conventional tests in attempting to identify types of intelligence in children. Formal tests that require children to answer questions orally, fill in blanks, or do other paper and pencil tasks, tend to favor students who are strong in linguistic and logical-mathematical abilities while discriminating against others who are weak in these areas but strong in one or more of the other areas.

Unfortunately, the schools persist in this kind of assessment. The next chapter explores this question of testing in the schools, showing how formal tests severely limit our perceptions of a child's capabilities. It presents you with sound reasons for discarding most of the standardized test results used to evaluate your child, and offers practical alternatives for discovering and describing your child's learning potential and progress—in all seven kinds of intelligence.

CHAPTER 3

Testing for Failure:
The Formal Test Trap

*W*hile I was a learning disability specialist, a woman from the school district's diagnostic center came one day to visit my special class. She brought with her a nine-year-old girl who shyly held her hand and hid behind her. This child had spent the previous six weeks undergoing extensive testing. "She's a nonverbal child," the lady from the diagnostic center emphatically told me. A couple of days later, Sally was a student in my class. Within two or three hours, she easily became one of the loudest, most verbal children in the room.

Why was the diagnostician so "off" in her evaluation of this child? Was it just a bad guess? I think not. I'd say instead that the lady was so wrapped up in the technicalities of formal testing that she failed to see the real Sally. In the same way, test givers across the country dehumanize millions of children by focusing on scores and percentiles instead of on their rich and complex lives.

The Tyranny of Testing

Twenty years ago, Banesh Hoffmann told a shocked country about the "tyranny of testing" in his classic book of the same name. His book and others that followed stirred up much controversy, leading the National Education Association in 1976 to recommend the elimination of group standardized intelligence, aptitude, and achievement tests. However, the dust seems to have settled from this uprising and the testing industry today appears more powerful than ever. The National Education Association has completely changed its stand and now "recognizes the need for periodic comprehensive testing for evaluation and diagnosis of student progress." No wonder, since it would have taken a major miracle to eliminate testing. Last year teachers gave over 500 million standardized tests to children and adults across the country.

A look at some of the individual items from these tests illustrates the ambiguities that a child must confront during evaluation time. A widely used achievement test asks the child to choose the correct item: "Something you see in your sleep is a . . . dream, fairy, wish, dread." Most normal children will have seen all of the above at one time or another in their slumber. Another well-known achievement test asks the child to circle the correct word: "An idea is a . . . picture, laugh, thought." For the spatially gifted child—who thinks in images and pictures—the first response would be most natural, but the last word would be the only response marked as correct. One of the most well-known intelligence tests for children asks: "What are you supposed to do if you find someone's wallet or pocketbook in a store?" and gives one point for the answer "call a radio or TV station" but no points for "just lay it up on the counter" or "wouldn't take it." This test is supposed to come up with some objective measure of intelligence, but in one study, ninety-nine school psychologists independently scored the test from identical records, and came up with IQs ranging from 63 to 117 for the same person.

Few people realize that the tests being used today in our nation's schools represent the end result of a historical process that has its origins in racial and cultural bigotry. Many of the founding fathers of the modern testing industry— including Lawrence Terman (creator of the Stanford-Binet IQ test) and Carl Brigham (the developer of the Scholastic Aptitude Test)—advocated eugenics, or the systematic control of hereditary characteristics to achieve racial superiority.

They saw testing as one way of achieving their aims. According to Harvard professor Steven Jay Gould in his acclaimed book *The Mismeasure of Man,* these tests were influential in legitimizing forced sterilization of allegedly "defective" individuals in some states and in keeping immigrants out of the United States at a time when they were fleeing the Nazi menace in Europe during the 1930s.

Such narrow-minded thinking appears shocking to us today. Yet psychologists still use test results to argue for the intellectual superiority of one race over another. And as David Owen points out in his book *None of the Above: Behind the Myth of Scholastic Aptitude,* tests like the SAT continue to favor certain social classes even as they close the door of educational opportunity to members of other groups. On the basis of test scores, the powers that be channel students into different "tracks" that determine their educational futures, and by virtue of the training they receive, chart their ultimate vocational destiny. While competency needs to be evaluated, the question remains whether formal testing is the best way of going about accomplishing this goal.

A New Breed of Tests

Mass testing of children on achievement and aptitude tests and widespread screening of children on IQ tests has gone on for fifty years. But now a whole new breed of individual tests and diagnostic instruments have arrived on the scene that threaten to make Banesh Hoffmann's dire pronouncements of testing tyranny look tame by comparison. One book lists over 300 separate tests for diagnosing learning problems, and this represents only a fraction of the total number used by psychologists and teachers.

This new diagnostic era of assessment would be a bright spot on the educational horizon if these tests really helped children. Unfortunately, it appears that most of them are worthless in identifying learning problems. Gerald Coles, assistant professor of psychiatry at Rutgers Medical School, put it succinctly: "We don't know what these tests measure." He made that statement after examining dozens of studies that evaluated the ten leading tests for learning disabilities. His examination turned up numerous flaws in test construction, including the use of poor subject selection and faulty research design. The tests may have *looked* good, but they failed to provide any useful information about how children actually learn.

These diagnostic tests—like their kin the intelligence and achievement tests—have little to do with the real lives of children. One test asks children to read out loud nonsense words like "twib," "expram," and "fubwit" in order to test their ability to sound out words. Another test requires children to repeat orally long lists of random numbers to get a sense of their memory skills. Still another test wants children to agree to the statements "bo/le is bottle" and "da/y is daddy," before going on to further questions to determine if they can hear the syllables that make up a whole word. Most of these tests demand that children do things they've never done before, would never choose to do on their own, and will never do again. Yet on the basis of their performance, these tests classify children as either normal or disabled learners.

It's no wonder then that children aren't crazy about taking tests of this kind. Test anxiety, confusion, and doubt are only some of the emotional snares that confront youngsters referred for an evaluation because of learning problems in the classroom. This stress is compounded when children perceive the tester as an alien force in their lives. A Maryland mother wrote me about her eight-year-old daughter's testing experience: "Tammy had a 'language-learning' evaluation yesterday. The woman was so cold and brittle in her manner that I think Tammy was positively heroic to answer questions for her for an hour and a half."

Testing is no picnic for children even when the tester is sympathetic. A New York teacher comments after giving an

eight-year-old boy one of the most widely used individualized diagnostic tests in the country: "It was very obvious
. . . that he did not like taking the [test] at all. Although he
didn't say so, it was pretty obvious by his facial expressions
that he was being pretty severely stressed. At the end, I felt
a need to explain the test to him, so I explained why I had
spent some time with him and asked if he had any questions.
He didn't have any questions. His only statement was, 'I
couldn't do it. I don't know the words.' Not crying, but very
upset." By putting stress on children in this way, tests do a
disservice to the deeper emotional needs of these youngsters, and serve the needs of the test makers instead. For, by
manufacturing disability in the assessment room, test makers are creating a whole new generation of "disabled" individuals who must now have their problems "remediated"
by fancy educational programs, often created by the test
makers themselves.

The Myth of the "Objective Test"

The child who shows up in the assessment
room exposes himself to a host of testing side effects that
may bias the results. Through a series of nonverbal cues, the
tester often unconsciously manipulates the results. This
testing room side effect, sometimes referred to as *the Clever
Hans phenomenon,* was named after a trick horse who could
perform astounding feats like computing numbers and spelling words in front of an amazed audience. It turned out that
Clever Hans' trainer had worked out a complex system of
gestures and cues—invisible to the audience—which the
horse responded to on command.

The tester, usually lacking the awareness of a horse
trainer, nevertheless may unintentionally manipulate the
child's behavior for good or ill. Already having some idea of
why the child has been referred for evaluation, he carries a
subliminal set of expectations concerning how the child will

perform. This works against the child referred for learning problems, since the tester will be on the lookout for any signs of difficulty and may unconsciously reinforce wrong answers or fail to give the child opportunities to perform well.

Whatever the outcome, it's clear that these assessments do not objectively test a child's ability. As San Diego State University sociologist Hugh Mehan points out in his book *Handicapping the Handicapped*, "Treating test results as social facts obscures the constitutive process by which testers and students jointly produce answers in individual tests." Mehan and his colleagues also observed the way learning disability specialists use a "test until find" approach in their work, where testers administer assessments to a child until they locate a suspected disability—at which time they stop testing and label the child. If they don't locate a disability after two or three tests, they administer up to fifteen or twenty other tests until they either find a disability or exhaust their entire battery. This way of working with children encourages fault-finding and minimizes the chances of discovering strengths and abilities.

In some cases, it's a practical necessity for school districts to find disabilities in their children. They receive almost twice as much money from federal and state sources for a learning disabled child than for a normal child. However, state and federal guidelines also place a ceiling on the number of children who can be identified as learning disabled. So when a school district hits its ceiling, they're no longer as eager to label. Mehan observed how one school district reached a ceiling point in March, which prompted a memo from the director of pupil personnel services to "refer only severe and obvious cases." The average number of referrals dropped by almost half. This means the learning disabled child in September may not be disabled in June because the school ran out of money. Tests in this case become instruments for fiscal management rather than objective measures of a child's abilities.

The Percentile Nightmare

Tests are supposed to give parents and teachers information about how children are progressing in their learning. Instead, they tend to reduce children and all of their thoughts, feelings, behaviors, and achievements to a handful of percentiles, rankings, letter grades, and fancy-sounding labels. For example, many achievements tests have a grade point level as their final score. One of the tests I gave as a teacher—the Wide Range Achievement Test (WRAT)—had children read a list of words, spell another list of words, and do a few math problems. On the basis of this quick procedure, children received scores such as 2.5 (second grade, fifth month) or 3.7 (third grade, seventh month) for each subject. An unsuspecting observer—including many parents—would think that a child was doing second or third grade work on the basis of this test. Yet it only took *five errors* out of forty-one spelling words to move from 5.0 to 3.9, a drop in the mind of the parent from fifth grade work to third grade work. Such test results tell us nothing about how the child spells or misspells words, whether the child misspells words in writing compositions, if the child enjoys spelling, or any number of other important questions related to the child's actual learning experience.

The WRAT is popular because it's so simple and quick to administer. Teachers can sit the child down and in a few minutes get scores on all the basic skills. Our school district regularly used the WRAT to write specific goals for children in special education: "Johnny will improve in spelling over the next ten months from a 3.2 score as measured on the WRAT to a 4.0." This sounds good but what it really means is that Johnny will be able to spell two or three more words on this little test that he takes every year.

Some tests carry this penchant for speed to absurd limits. One popular test gives teachers the opportunity to play medical doctor by administering a neurological screening to a child in twenty minutes. Computers are also a big part of the picture in this hurry to assess. One software program assures us that a teacher with no previous computer experience will be able to create in less than fifteen minutes a complete IEP (individualized educational program) that is in compliance with federal special education laws. Administrators understandably need to be concerned with efficiency. But what are we doing to children when we reduce them to statistics and computer printout sheets?

Testing also boxes children in with convenient labels couched in scientific-sounding educational jargon. The learning specialist says that the child who is not paying attention during the testing session suffers from "attention deficit disorder." The child who has difficulty remembering test instructions has "poor auditory sequential skills." Children get saddled with diagnostic terms such as *dyslexia, dysgraphia, dyscalculia,* and the like, making it sound as if they suffer from very rare and exotic diseases. Yet the word *dyslexia* is just Latin bafflegab, or jargon, for "trouble with words." Any parent who has a ten-year-old child struggling in a first grade primer could have told you that.

Using numbers and jargon from educational testing to describe students serves another purpose as well. Coming from the mouths of psychologists and learning specialists during a parent meeting, this practice carries with it a special aura of expertise and authority. After all, who could possibly question the conclusions of a psychologist that "Martha has visuo-spatial dysfunction as indicated by her score of 7 on the object assembly subtest of the WISC-R"?

Mehan points out that statements made by psychologists and learning specialists during parent conferences were often followed by silence—suggesting unquestioned acceptance of their conclusions. Parents who shared what they knew about their children, on the other hand, were usually pummelled with questions, casting doubt on the truth of their statements. Parents deserve better treatment than this. Yet testing continues to reinforce the schools' authority by placing the almighty statistic on a pedestal far beyond the reach of all but the most trained professional. Common sense and real-life experience function like menial serfs in this educational hierarchy.

Protecting Your Child from Formal Testing

Despite the many shortcomings described above, our national confidence in testing seems to be stronger than ever. We see this unquestioning attitude in every headline that blares out, "National Math Scores Show Third Straight Yearly Increase," or "IQ Scores Higher in Suburban Communities." What can a parent do to help counteract the dehumanizing qualities of formal testing? Given the reality of deeply rooted cultural and financial forces working to keep the testing industry as powerful as ever, you may want to consider some ways to protect your child from the worst aspects of formal testing.

Examining School Records

Don't be pushed around by test scores that teachers and administrators present to you about your child. One Vermont private school director recommends that parents of incoming children destroy all previous school test records, as these serve only to distort the child's true capabilities. While you can't exactly do this if your child is in public school, you can refuse to give these scores the sort of importance that they receive in school circles. Also, federal law gives parents the right to inspect confidential files, to request in writing that certain materials be taken out, and if school officials refuse, to request a hearing on the matter. Parents also can insert into school records written statements objecting to the material that is there and present additional information on their child.

Alternative Evaluation Methods

Encourage your school to rely more on alternative methods of evaluation in assessing your child. Possibilities include criterion-referenced testing, informal testing, observation, and documentation.

Criterion-Referenced Testing. These assessments don't statistically compare children to each other. Rather, they report on those skills that your child has actually mastered, as well as on those objectives your child has yet to achieve. By making test results concrete and positive (Johnny can multiply two-digit numbers, do fifty push-ups in ten minutes, use a table of contents), they give constructive information that a parent or teacher can use to take a child to even higher levels of achievement.

Informal Testing. These are tests that you make up as you go along to find out whatever you want to know about a child. No need to purchase expensive test kits and fill out elaborate testing forms. If you're wondering whether your child can subtract or not, you don't have to go out and get an elaborate psychoeducational test battery. Just grab a piece of paper or a miniature chalkboard, write down a couple of subtraction problems, and let your child loose on them. What is particularly good about informal testing is that there is less concern for the test results and more concern for the test process.

What kind of strategy does your child engage in when he subtracts? Does he count on his fingers? Does he remember to borrow? Ask him to explain what borrowing means. Does he understand or is he just using a rule that he memorized?

These and other questions can give you a rich collection of data about your child's problem-solving abilities vastly superior to the information that most tests give.

Ask your child's teacher how much he or she relies on informal testing. During parent conferences, do you hear about your child only in terms of test scores and jargon? Or do you really receive meaningful information about the way in which your child learns? If so, the teacher probably uses informal assessment at least some of the time.

Observation. The trouble with most of the highly sophisticated tests used by learning specialists these days is that they have little to do with the child's own personal reality. The child is diagnosed as deficient in auditory memory skills yet is able to tell you a long story that someone told him a week before. This happens because the test suggesting a deficiency involved repeating back to the examiner nonsense syllables or random digits—activities that are without meaning to the child. They ought to call deficiency in this area by another name—*auditory yawnitis dysfunction*—"the inability to remember meaningless and boring information."

Observation gives a parent or teacher the opportunity to see children in meaningful contexts doing things that have a real connection to their lives. Anything observed at home or at school in the course of a day—whether it shows a strength or a weakness—can be important information. It's truly appalling how often I've looked into the school records of a child only to see endless pages of test results smothering a few vague sentences here and there describing something about the child ("Susan tries hard," or "Peter is cooperative"). Keep a daily journal of your own observations and encourage your child's teacher to do the same.

Documentation. This method of evaluation lets you keep track of your child's school performance in concrete ways. Some of the "documents" you or your child's teacher can keep include writing samples, cassette tapes of your child reading a book, pictures your child has drawn, snapshots or videotape of your child engaged in a learning activity, or samples of things your child has made or done. These materials, when assembled as a "portfolio" of learning accomplishments, or summarized in a report, show much more of the real child than a dry collection of test scores.

Assessment As a Positive Experience

Whether at home or at school, see that evaluation becomes a supportive educational experience for your child. A while back, I needed to find children on whom to practice my own testing skills for my doctoral degree. After locating some neighborhood children, I discovered that I couldn't pay them to take the tests. Their feelings about testing were too negative. The best way to make evaluation fun for children is by making it part of what they already enjoy doing. I remember having positive feelings as a child while taking the presidential fitness tests out on the playground because I was doing things that I would have chosen to do anyway—climb the parallel bars, do chin-ups, and run across the field.

If you want to know how well children read, spare them from formal reading tests. Instead, sit with them and their favorite story book and informally assess how well they read. Instead of a test on fractions, bake bread with them and discover as they work with measurements how well they're able to compute. This method of evaluation lets you see children applying their learning in concrete ways, rather than demonstrating it in some irrelevant and disconnected way on a paper-and-pencil test.

Discussing Test Results with Your Child

Make sure your child gets direct feedback at home and at school on assessment results.   Children who have trouble learning may go through a five-hour diagnostic battery at school and then end up in remedial groups or special education classes without ever being told anything about the test scores that resulted in their changing programs. Even in regular classes, children work for hours on materials they will never see again. Take time, preferably right after any assessing that you or your child's teacher has done, to discuss the results with your child. Better yet, see that your child has the opportunity to receive self-feedback, by providing her with scoring keys, self-correcting materials, or other information about where to go for the answers. Let her keep charts and graphs of her learning progress in quantifiable areas, and diaries or journals to keep track of special achievements.

Evaluation of school progress doesn't need to be tyrannical. Neither does it have to serve as a way of sorting children into various kinds of disabilities. Ideally, there should be no dividing line between testing and learning. As you teach your child anything, you gather information about what she knows and doesn't know. Moreover, you use that information to determine what next steps to take in the learning process. By seeing evaluation as linked to the process of learning—and not as a way of deciding who can and can't learn—we can make it a positive force in our children's lives.

Teaching to the Tests

Unfortunately, some teachers take the learning-evaluation link too literally. Pressured to show high test scores, they engage in "teaching to the tests," constructing the curriculum around the test, rather than the other way around as it should be done. Testifying at a National Institute of Education hearing on minimum competency testing in 1981, Deborah Meier, the principal of a public school in Manhattan, observed that reading instruction in the New York City schools actually amounted to instruction in taking reading tests. George Madaus, director of the Center for the Study of Testing, Evaluation, and Educational Policy at Boston College, commented: "In typical reading classes, students read commercially prepared materials made up of dozens of short paragraphs about which they then answer questions. The materials they use are designed to look exactly like the tests they will take in the spring. . . . When synonyms and antonyms were dropped from a test on word comprehension, teachers promptly dropped the commercially prepared materials that stressed them."

This approach to testing and teaching threatens to turn our nation's children into a generation of cynical fill-in-the-blankers rather than truly independent thinkers who possess a deep thirst for knowledge. We'll explore this tragedy more fully in the next chapter when we examine how teachers bore students to an early intellectual death with textbooks, worksheets, and other stale instructional methods.

CHAPTER 4

Dysteachia: The Real Reason Your Child Isn't Thriving in School

It's been said that if we taught children to speak the way we teach them to read, we'd have a nation of stutterers. This is just another way of saying that our schools are selling millions of kids short by putting them into remedial groups or writing them off as underachievers, when in reality they are disabled only by poor teaching methods. We hear so much about the learning disabled child in the news media. It's probably truer to say that these children are "worksheet disabled," "curriculum dysfunctional," or "dysteachic." And there are millions of other children out there who don't show any of the overt signs of "pedagogical illness" who secretly are suffering from teaching strategies inappropriate to their real needs.

The schools fail our children when they limit their teaching methods to lectures, textbooks, worksheets, and quizzes. They create learning problems when they focus on a narrow band of isolated skills representing only two of Howard Gardner's seven kinds of intelligence. They stifle the learning potential of children when they channel them into groups, "tracks," and special classes. They dampen the thirst for knowledge in all children by teaching them things that have little relevance to their personal lives.

The Four Ts That Kill Learning: Talk, Textbooks, Task Analysis, and Tracking

Enter a typical classroom, says John Goodlad in *A Place Called School*, and the chances are better than 50/50 that you will observe a group of thirty or so children seated at tables or desks working quietly on worksheets or workbooks, preparing for assignments, or listening to a teacher lecturing to them from the front of the classroom. These practices continue despite research that fails to support their effectiveness as learning methods. The children in our schools are victims of several widespread educational malpractices.

Too much teacher talk. Children listen to teachers' explanations and lectures about one-fifth of the school day in an average classroom, according to Goodlad's study. This in itself isn't so bad, but most of this "frontal teaching" takes place in the absence of any true interaction with students. Teachers talk *at* the students, not to them. When teachers ask questions, frequently they're of the "fill-in-the-blank" kind, requiring specific, short responses from students. Student responses are met with impersonal or automatic replies, such as "all right." Teachers rarely ask students for their own opinions or engage them in any kind of meaningful dialogue designed to sharpen thinking abilities. Educator Leslie Hart says that teachers generally speak to only about one-third of the class anyway. Teachers need quick and accurate responses from children. In their rush to get through the material, they call on those who can produce correct answers, largely writing off the rest of the class in the process.

Overuse of textbooks. Textbooks constitute a $1.5 billion business annually and can be found in just about every classroom across the country. They're widely used because they deliver information in a tightly controlled and highly efficient manner, perfectly designed for a bureaucracy like the schools. Whether they actually teach children anything meaningful is another matter. P. Kenneth Komoski, executive director of educational products for the Information Exchange Institute in Water Mill, New York, comments: "Most textbooks tell about a discipline in order to 'cover it,' rather than engaging the learner in the skills and processes of that discipline to a level of mastery." There's no personal "voice" in a textbook that students can learn from since most texts are assembled by editorial committees from among numerous authors. Texts contain mainly declarative sentences, speaking "the truth" from some high and impersonal place. As a result, students get little sense of the complexities—and realities—of the topic they are studying.

Since textbooks are currently under fire from all sides of the political and cultural spectrum, publishers take special pains to avoid controversy. This results in a very bland product that never really touches the actual concerns and feelings of the students they were designed to serve. The books themselves resist interaction in a very literal sense—students are not allowed to write in them and must turn them in at the end of the year. It's no wonder then that students find textbooks dull and disconnected from their lives.

Overemphasis on teaching specific skills.   There used to be a time when a child went to school and learned to read by reading. Nowadays, however, children may spend much of their reading time learning to master hundreds of specific skills before actually settling down to read a good book. This fragmented approach to learning has its origins in the concept of "task analysis." Followers of task analysis believe you must break down an activity into its parts, and then learn the separate parts, before you can master the total activity. This approach may work well for a team of electrical engineers, but it fails in the classroom. Teachers and children end up spending so much time focusing on the parts that they lose sight of the whole.

The bedrock of this educational malpractice is the worksheet or ditto. Teachers run off mass quantities of these items on duplicating machines or provide children with ready-made packages of them in workbooks. Each sheet is supposed to develop a specific skill, such as the ability to recognize the "sh" sound in reading or the capacity to add two-digit numbers in math. Students must fill in the blank, circle the correct item, draw a line from a word to its corresponding picture, or in some other way successfully complete the task. Teachers love worksheets because they provide simple and clear results of a student's progress. Yet parents shouldn't be deceived by this simplistic approach to learning. Anne Adams of the Duke University Reading Center cautions: "Parents are told that 'Johnny knows this skill, but not this one," and they fly into a panic. What they should be looking for is independent reading as early as possible. They should have a sense that sometimes these skills lessons kill independent reading." See *Insult to Intelligence* by Frank Smith for a scathing indictment of skill teaching in America.

Overreliance on grouping children by achievement or ability. Grouping begins almost as soon as a child walks in the door on that first day of school, when the teacher begins administering screening tests to determine achievement levels. Based on the results, Betty gets into the "golden eagle" reading group and Harry ends up in the "chicken hawks." Ten years later, Betty heads toward college in the academic track of her high school, while Harry plods along in the vocational track towards some fuzzy destiny as a busboy or burger flipper. Teachers argue that grouping by ability allows more efficient instruction and avoids frustrating either slow or fast children who aren't learning at the same rate as their peers.

Yet, these justifications aren't supported by the data. Research suggests that students in ability groups don't progress as quickly as those in heterogeneous, or mixed, groups. Moreover, those children who end up in the low or slow groups definitely get the short end of the stick academically. There's less emphasis on enrichment and more focus on drill- and rote-learning in these classes. Students in the low tracks see teachers as more punitive and less concerned about them. Their self-esteem is lower, their drop out rate is higher, and their general progress is slower than in the high tracks, where a child may advance up to five times more quickly. One might argue that this is the result of the quality of the students rather than the grouping itself, yet studies have shown that when a child of so-called average ability is placed in one of the low tracks, he does less well than if he'd been placed in a mixed group. The low group seems to function according to the laws of entropy, sucking children down to its own level of diminished expectations. More frighteningly, it shapes the destinies of schoolchildren who, given a different setting, might have gone on to develop more of their true potential.

Special Education: An Ecology of Its Own

A new kind of grouping came into being over the past fifteen years with the spread of special education programs for the learning disabled. There was a time when special education mainly served the needs of children with severe physical or developmental handicaps. However, it underwent a major change with congressional passage of the Education for All Handicapped Children Act in 1975. Funds then became available to schools to meet the needs of the so-called learning disabled. As a result, the percentage of children labeled learning disabled doubled in six years, from 21.5 percent of all special education students in 1977 to 40.9 percent in 1983. Currently, almost 2 million children are in these special LD classes.

For the most part, these programs simply heap upon children more concentrated doses of what they're already failing at in the regular classroom: more worksheets, duller textbooks, and stricter teacher control. However, LD programs also create an entirely new ecology of their own with their own tests, their own specialized jargon, and their own educational programs. The most common of these instructional methods up until about five years ago was something called sensory-motor training. This required children among other things to walk balance beams, put together puzzles, trace designs, and ride around on scooter boards. Today these activities are rarely used, because the research suggested they were worthless in helping children learn to read, write, or compute.

Also ineffective were so-called remedial reading programs. Norman and Margaret Silberberg, two Minnesota psychologists, pointed out that the research supporting these methods initially showed a large increase in achievement scores over groups of students who did not receive remediation. However, when one looked at the results over a longer period of time, differences between the remedial and the control groups "washed out."

Like prisons, LD classrooms often serve as proving grounds for misbehavior, where a small number of children referred for severe emotional problems pass along their instability to the rest of the students. Carl Milofsky, a California sociologist who spent several months in classes for the educationally handicapped wrote of his experience, "It was clear that, if anything, the special class made students more rebellious and harder to handle."

Meanwhile, special class teachers, snowed under by discipline problems, also have their hands full with all the red tape required by federal and state laws. One parent who participated in a special education conference remarked: "What I remember of that meeting was sitting there looking at all the forms she was filling out. I just thought, 'I don't see how they're getting anything done here because it seems to me all they're doing is filling out forms.' "

A more serious problem with many LD programs is that by removing children from the "mainstream" of regular classroom life, there's a greater likelihood that these youngsters will fall further behind their peers. Lee Ann Trusdell of the City University of New York, in a study of remedial programs in New York City, observed that many students were receiving instruction in special classes that was totally unrelated to what was being taught in regular classes. As these children become more disconnected from their home-room classes, it becomes that much harder for them to return. In fact, many of these youngsters, initially referred to special education for minor remediation, soon make a career out of their disability and slip more deeply into the LD labyrinth. Jeanne Westin interviewed teachers in *The Coming Parent Revolution* who commented: "Few EH [educationally handicapped] children ever make it back into the mainstream of education. . . . They're gone. . . . These are the kids we don't save."

The most devastating result of the whole learning disability myth, however, is that it has made it so much easier for teachers to toss any child who isn't learning the material in the prescribed way out of their normal classroom. As a federal study on labeling once stated, "The term learning disability has appeal because it implies a specific neurological condition for which no one can be held particularly responsible." Teachers can go on teaching in the same stale way. Children remaining in the regular classroom get the message. Keep quiet and do your work—even though it bores you to death—or suffer the consequences of special education.

Beyond Boredom: How Children Actually Learn

While most schools operate on the basis of the "mug-jug" theory—where the teacher as jug pours knowledge into the student's mug—the best evidence we have suggests that learning for children is like a series of small scientific revolutions. Thomas Kuhn, professor of the history of science at Princeton and author of *The Structure of Scientific Revolutions*, points out that a scientific revolution goes through a series of specific stages. At first, a ruling paradigm or world view—such as the belief that the earth is flat—holds sway among the people. Confirming evidence—including the observation that the world *appears* flat—is quickly assimilated into this belief system. Any contradictory evidence is viewed with skepticism and rejected. Gradually, however, contrary evidence begins to pile up until such time that it can no longer be ignored. At this moment, the revolution occurs, and people suddenly change their basic view of things—in this case, they shift their perspective and begin to see the earth as round.

Children go through a similar process. They construct what world-renowned child development researcher Jean Piaget called "schemes" or mini-world views about a wide range of things. At first these schemes are of "the earth is flat" variety. John Holt shared one of these primitive beliefs from his own classroom experience when he observed that some children felt the higher you went up the number line, the denser or closer together the numbers got. Children do not easily let go of these beliefs. They will continue to resist new input into their fixed schemes until such time as they are developmentally ready and the evidence presented from the outside world becomes overwhelming. Piaget would say it is then that they start to accommodate or change their old beliefs so as to effectively assimilate or take in new information. The equivalent of a scientific revolution goes on inside their heads. In a word, they learn.

In order for this to happen, children need to be presented with environments that challenge their old erroneous belief systems and present them with a wide range of methods and materials for exploring new, more accurate and useful beliefs. Unfortunately, the schools generally don't do this. Instead, they tend to perpetuate fixed ways of thinking by feeding children old, tired information, providing nothing new to challenge existing beliefs. Day after day youngsters fill in blanks, answer simple questions, and listen to boring lectures. They may gain a skill here or a shred of data there. But nothing changes fundamentally in their view of the world. No real learning takes place.

This impoverishment has its inevitable consequences in the brain. Mark Rosenzweig and his colleagues at the University of California, Berkeley, startled the world several years ago when they demonstrated the impact of the environment on brain structures in rats. They set up three different environments, including a standard laboratory cage with three rats, an impoverished environment with one rat in a bare cage, and an enriched environment with twelve rats living together in a large space fully equipped with playthings that were changed daily. All rats received adequate amounts of food and water. After they had lived in these environments for a time, their brains were dissected and measured. The rats in the enriched environment had cerebral cortexes of greater weight and thickness—in other words, larger brains—than the animals in either of the other two environments. While attempts to draw parallels to humans remain controversial, these studies suggest that most schools, in their present state, may not be the best places for children to develop their brain cells.

Children seem to have an intuitive sense of what kind of enriched environment they need to support their own neurological development. In Goodlad's study, they identified their preferred learning activities as building or drawing things, making collections, going on field trips, interviewing people, acting things out, and carrying out independent projects—in other words, participating in activities that engage all seven of the basic kinds of intelligence. Unfortunately, these activities were rarely observed in visits to over 1000 classrooms.

How to Get the Best Education for Your Child

The picture of education presented so far in this chapter is not a rosy one. Yet, parents can still get a high-quality education for their children if they are willing to inform themselves about the options available, and then take positive steps toward providing their children with a schooling environment that allows them to learn in their own way.

Look at your child's current educational setting and ask yourself whether it's providing what he really needs. To make this assessment, you need to visit your child's classroom, speak with his teacher, and spend some time talking with your child about his school experience. Here are some questions to ask:

About the Classroom

- Does it appear lively and energetic, or dull and lethargic?
- Is it filled with lots of inviting learning materials—art supplies, science materials, things to touch, stroke, manipulate, and wonder about—or is it bare except for a few dusty textbooks and ancient posters on the walls?
- Are children building, drawing, reading, collecting, writing, relating, experimenting, and creating, or are they working on skill sheets, studying textbooks, and listening to the teacher lecture?

- Are there a variety of spaces in the classroom for group discussion, physical movement, quiet study, and creative "messing around," or are there straight rows of desks, a few tables, and little else?

About the Teacher

- Does he invite opinion and dialogue or require quick and short answers to teacher-directed questions?
- Does he move around the classroom helping individual students or spend most of the time at the front of the room talking at everybody?
- When you speak with the teacher about your child, do you hear more about the accomplishments or the problems?
- Does he seem to have a wide range of methods for teaching any given skill or does he instead rely mainly on workbooks and textbooks?

About Your Child

- When you talk to your child about the class, do you feel his own sense of excitement toward learning, or do you instead get a feeling of quiet desperation or passive compliance?
- Does he seem to be learning for learning's sake, or to earn prizes, grades, stars, or praise?
- Is he getting an opportunity to express his unique strengths, talents, and abilities during the school day, or is there a lot of emphasis on his mistakes, disabilities, and underachievement?
- Is he treated like a human being with a personal way of learning or is he expected instead to learn in the same way as everybody else?

Parents' answers to these questions, and others like them, will help to determine whether or not their children are getting an education based on their individual needs. If you find your child's school environment is lacking—and many of you probably will—then consider some alternatives.

Five Options for Schooling Your Child

Option 1: Work to Create Change within Your Child's Current Schooling Situation

Meet with your child's teacher and discuss your concerns about the classroom. Be an advocate for your child, pointing out specific abilities, talents, or strengths that are being neglected at school and suggest ways in which these might be incorporated into the classroom day. Offer to serve as a volunteer in the class. Bring in innovative learning materials to enrich the classroom. Above all, work cooperatively and diplomatically. Teachers are under a lot of pressure these days and may feel like your sincere attempts to help your child are just another problem they have to confront. If the teacher sees your offers of assistance as an opportunity to lighten her own load, then you will probably succeed in changing the status quo for your child. However, if your efforts are met with stubborn resistance, consider another option.

Option 2: Move Your Child to Another Classroom, Another School, or Another District

If your child should happen to be in a "brain antagonistic" classroom, and all your efforts to change things fail, then just as you would transplant a withering plant into more fertile soil, you might consider a more hospitable climate (friendlier teacher, more exciting classroom) within your child's present school or at another school in the area. In their classic book *The Myth of the Hyperactive Child*, Diane Divoky and Peter Schrag report how in one community

> the parents get a note from the school nurse: "Your son is hyperactive. He doesn't sit still in school. Please see a physician." The parents send the child to another school with another teacher and the "problem" is never mentioned again. In a suburb in Cleveland, a boy referred to a class for the learning disabled performs even worse in the judgment of the teachers than he did in the regular classroom; in desperation, they send him to another regular classroom and he begins to read.

Giving your child a new start in this way may help him to avoid being caught in a vicious cycle of learning failure.

Option 3: Send Your Child to a Private Alternative School

There are thousands of alternative schools around the country that honor individual learning styles and provide rich environments addressing all seven kinds of intelligence. Two approaches that account for many of these schools are the Montessori and Waldorf systems. Montessori schools were developed in the early 1900s by an Italian physician, Maria Montessori, and number in the thousands worldwide. They emphasize sensory-motor experience, practical and academic learning based on the use of concrete learning materials, and a real respect for the integrity of the child. Waldorf education, founded by German philosopher Rudolf Steiner in the 1920s, uses an artistic approach in teaching reading, history, math, science, and literature. Also, it provides instruction in crafts, dance, drama, and music.

Hundreds of other independent alternative schools exist around the nation that allow children to learn at their own pace and in their own way. One mother told me how her first grade child was referred to a special education class in a public school for learning and behavioral problems. "Then the behavior problems at home started. Suddenly Tim didn't want to go to school anymore, hated school, was miserable at school. He hated the teacher. It was during that year one morning he ran away." At the end of first grade, she took him out of the public schools and placed him in a private school that emphasized both Montessori and Waldorf approaches. She comments: "They took all the pressure off. He was like a different child. He loved school, he loved learning, he couldn't wait to get to school. It was as if we were looking at a different child." While alternative schools can be expensive or inconveniently located, they may be worth the extra cost and time if they save you the hassle of living with a frustrated or dissatisfied learner. You might also consider banding together with other parents to create your own cooperative alternative school.

Option 4: Consider Teaching Your Child at Home

A growing number of parents whose children have suffered at the hands of public or private education are discovering that the best thing they can do for their children is to educate them at home. Home schooling has become popular in the past few years largely through the efforts of individuals such as the late John Holt, author of *Teach Your Own* and Raymond and Dorothy Moore, who wrote *School Can Wait* and *Home Style Teaching.* Current estimates of home schooling parents around the country range from ten thousand into the hundreds of thousands.

I've heard from many parents who've experienced success with this approach. One mother in Georgia writes: "My oldest child was in sixth grade and couldn't read. After home schooling her for two years, she now reads adult-level books." A New Hampshire mother whose fourteen-year-old daughter failed in several different programs in public school wrote me after a few months of home schooling: "her mind started getting more creative, she demonstrated more patience in her projects, and now she loves to read." While this option is impractical if both parents work outside of the home, increasingly families are discovering that it may be worth it to modify their lifestyles so as to provide a better education for their offspring.

Option 5: Use the Special Education Laws to Your Child's Advantage

Current federal law states that every handicapped child in the country has the right to an appropriate education. Many parents whose children aren't learning in the schools have chosen to have their children tested and declared "learning handicapped" to make them eligible for special LD programs. While there's often nothing "special" about these programs, and they frequently cause more problems than they solve, occasionally it happens that the most exciting classroom in a school is the resource room or "special class." This can be a viable option for some parents, since the ratio of teacher to students is small and teachers have been instructed to work with individual learning styles. However it should only be used as a last resort in my opinion, since it requires stigmatizing your child with a handicapping label.

On the positive side, the laws favor parent and child. By law parents have the right to participate fully in every stage of the process that leads to placing their children in special programs. They have the right to an independent evaluation if they disagree with the school's diagnosis. They can request that specific approaches or materials be used in teaching their children. They can take their case to a court of law should the school fail to provide the kind of education they feel their children need.

If you choose the special education route, make sure you inform yourself fully beforehand of all the procedures and potential pitfalls. The book *Negotiating the Special Education Maze* by Winifred Anderson, Stephen Chitwood, and Deidre Hayden may be helpful in guiding you through this labyrinth. Before you choose this option, read *The Magic Feather: The Truth About Special Education* by Lori and Bill Granger. The Granger's son, Alec, was labeled retarded even though he read above grade level and had many other talents and skills (he now attends a Montessori school). Reading *The Magic Feather* may cause you to have second thoughts about subjecting your child to the testing and labeling that goes along with being in special education.

Beyond these suggestions, there are more far-reaching things you can do to improve the lot of children in the schools. Get involved in your local PTA, attend school board meetings, and support school board candidates who favor child-centered approaches to education. Finally, even if you feel you can't change the way your child is being educated at school, you can still have a tremendous impact at home during the eighteen hours that your child *isn't* in school every day. The next chapter will suggest ways in which you can create learning activities at home tailor-made to your child's specific learning needs.

Learning in Their Own Way: Giving Children at Home What They May Not Be Getting at School

One of the greatest shortcomings of the schools seems to be their gross inflexibility when it comes to teaching a subject or skill. Teachers present the material in one way—usually through some combination of lectures, blackboard lessons, textbooks, and worksheets—and if children don't get it, then it's *their* problem, not the teachers'. But as we've seen, children learn in a number of ways and need to be taught *their* way if it's really going to sink in. Let's explore how you can create an optimum learning environment in your home suited to your child's particular learning needs.

Finding the Right Way to Motivate Your Child

Many parents and teachers feel that all you need to do is "motivate" children in order to get them to learn. This is quite true, but it doesn't tell you how to go about doing it. As you'll see from the many ideas in this chapter, there are any number of ways to do this, depending upon your child's personal learning style.

Before you read further, go back and re-read Chapter 2, making sure to review the descriptions of the seven types of intelligence to help you identify your child's personal learning style. Remember that every child possesses all seven kinds of intelligence in varying degrees. Your child's personal learning style will consist of a combination of these. As you read through the rest of this chapter—with its many practical activities, techniques, and methods for learning— don't make the mistake of identifying your child as, say, a "spatial child" and use only those suggestions. Your child may benefit from specific activities found in all seven intelligence groups.

Learning the linguistic way. Children strong in this area learn best by saying, hearing, and seeing words. The best ways of motivating them at home include talking with them, providing them with lots of books, records, and tapes of the spoken word, and creating opportunities for writing. Supply them with tools for word-making, including tape recorders for oral language, and typewriters, word processors, label-makers, and printing sets for writing activities. As a family, read books together, have evenings of storytelling, and maybe even create a family newsletter that they can edit. Take them to places where words are important, including libraries, bookstores, newspaper bureaus, and publishing houses.

Learning the logical-mathematical way. Children strong in this variety of intelligence learn by forming concepts and looking for abstract patterns and relationships. Provide them with concrete materials they can experiment with, lots of time to explore new ideas, patience in answering their probing questions, and logical explanations for the answers that you do give. Supply them with games like chess and Go, logical puzzles, science kits, and a computer. They may also enjoy creating collections of things they can classify and categorize (stamps, coins, butterflies, and so on). As a family, play mystery games like Clue that require deductive logic and go to places that encourage scientific thinking including science museums, computer fairs, and electronics exhibitions.

Learning the spatial way. Children who excel in this area learn visually and need to be taught through images, pictures, and color. They can best be motivated through media such as films, slides, videos, diagrams, maps, and charts. Give them opportunities to draw and paint. Provide them with cameras, telescopes, compasses, and three-dimensional building supplies such as Lego blocks or D-stix. As a family, engage them in visualization games, tell vivid stories, and share dreams together. Visit architectural landmarks, planetariums, art museums, and other places where spatial awareness reigns supreme.

Learning the kinesthetic way. Kids talented in this type of intelligence learn by touching, manipulating, and moving. They need learning activities that are kinetic, dynamic, and visceral. The best ways of motivating them are through role play, dramatic improvisation, creative movement, and activities of all kinds involving physical activity. Provide them with access to playgrounds, obstacle courses, hiking trails, swimming pools, and gymnasiums. Give them opportunities for fixing machines, building models, and getting involved in hands-on art activities such as carving wood and working with clay. Let them take care of small animals. As a family, play physical games together, participate in activities that involve lots of touching, visit sporting events, go on camping trips, and engage in other vigorous and interactive experiences.

Learning the musical way. Youngsters with musical intelligence learn through rhythm and melody. They can learn anything more easily if it is sung, tapped out, or whistled. Use metronomes, percussion instruments, or computerized sound systems as ways to help learn rote material. Let them study with their favorite music in the background if it seems to help. Provide them with access to records and tapes, musical instruments, and music lessons if they request them. As a family, sing and make music together, talk about the words to favorite songs, and go to places that highlight musical intelligence including operas, concerts, and musicals.

Learning the interpersonal way. Children gifted in this category learn best by relating and cooperating. They need to learn through dynamic interaction with other people. Give them opportunities to teach other children. Supply them with games of all kinds that they can share with their friends. Let them get involved in community activities—clubs, committees, after-school programs, and volunteer organizations. Have frequent family discussions and problem-solving sessions. Work together on group projects. Go together to family-oriented retreats and political, cultural, or social events of all kinds.

Learning the intrapersonal way. Children inclined in this direction learn best when left to themselves. These youngsters are self-motivating. Provide them with the chance to pursue independent study, self-paced instruction, and individualized projects and games. It's very important for them to have their own private space at home where they can work on hobbies and interests undisturbed and spend time in quiet introspection. In the same way, they need a special place out in nature—a tree house or fort, for example—where they can get away to think things over. Respect their privacy, let them know that it's okay to be independent, and provide them with the resources they need to help them pursue their particular interests. As a family, go on long quiet walks, read about heroes who stand out from the crowd, and worship or meditate together.

Now that you have a sense of some general principles regarding the different learning styles, let's put that knowledge to work and apply these ideas to specific things that you'd like your child to learn—beginning with reading.

Seven Roads to Reading Success

In 1955, Rudolf Flesch wrote a book that shocked millions of parents and sent ripples of alarm through American education. His book, *Why Johnny Can't Read,* indicted the nation's schools for teaching reading in a way that left many children confused and illiterate. Flesch observed that the schools primarily used the "look-say" method of instruction, requiring children to memorize whole words as a way of learning to read. According to Flesch, this approach was difficult for many children and an ineffective way of cracking the English code. What was his solution? Phonics. Rather than learning whole words, children needed to learn the sounds or *phonemes* that make up whole words. Now, thirty years later, his book has been reissued and continues to be immensely popular.

Meanwhile, phonics instruction has become the primary method of reading instruction in tens of thousands of schools across the country. Yet, according to some estimates, we have over a million teenagers leaving high school every year as functional illiterates, 8 million children currently in school suffering from significant reading problems, and many millions more either not reading up to their potential or not enjoying the experience once they do learn to read. Clearly, phonics is not the complete answer.

The fact of the matter is that phonics generally works just fine with most children gifted in linguistic intelligence. They are auditory learners who are very sensitive to the sounds of language. A reading approach based upon subtle sound differences (sh-, th-, f, . . .) capitalizes on their learning strengths. However, phonics alone may not work as well with children strong in other types of intelligence. That's why it's important for parents to understand that there's no magic formula for reading success that will apply to all children. The right reading program for your child is the one that makes best use of her personal learning style, and there are at least seven other approaches besides phonics that you can choose from.

Helping your child learn to read linguistically. Some children are strong in the oral aspects of linguistic intelligence—they're great storytellers—but may have trouble with the auditory demands of phonics or find all those phonics workbooks and basal readers too deadly dull. Oral learners need to approach reading through their own spoken language. Sit down with them and ask them to tell you a story, describe their day, recount a television program or talk about anything else. Write down every word they say. If you wish, you can tape record the session and later transcribe it. Then print the story in easy-to-read block letters or type it out on a primary-school typewriter with large-sized type. Staple the pages together with extra blank pages inserted for illustrations and sturdy cardboard sheets at the front and back for covers. If your child wants a more professional appearance, take the "book" to a copy store that does simple binding and have it bound for a dollar or two. These bound volumes of your child's oral language can become her very own personalized readers. If you've made a tape recording of the original text, then let her listen to the tape as she reads along.

Helping your child learn to read spatially. These children need to have visual cues in learning to read. One reading program—the *Peabody Rebus Reading Program*—uses primers containing pictures that stand for simple words, such as a picture of a bee to stand for "be," an eye to represent "I," and so forth. Other programs, like Caleb Gattegno's *Words in Color,* combine phonics instruction with color. See Chapter

7 for specific reading activities you can use that capitalize on imagination—another strength for spatially gifted children.

Helping your child learn to read kinesthetically. Youngsters strong in this intelligence need to write before they read. They must involve their bodies in the creation of letters and words before they can read them in a purely auditory and visual way. Provide them with frequent opportunities for free drawing, modeling, and painting before beginning more structured writing activities. Then, let them create letters and words in clay, sand, and paint, and use the typewriter or a computer since these tools capitalize on their heightened tactile sensitivity. Chapter 6 offers many other ideas for using the body in reading.

Helping your child learn to read musically. These children will learn to read if you find simple songs that they love and type or write out the lyrics in large print to use as their basic primer just as you did with the linguistically-inclined child. Also select simple poems and stories they can read or sing rhythmically. Buy book and cassette packages that combine story with song.

Helping your child learn to read logical-mathematically. Children with strengths in this area enjoy looking for patterns and regularities. Hence, reading programs based on word patterns ("the rat sat on the mat") may appeal to these children if they're given an opportunity to actively explore these patterns and create their own. Provide them with dice on which have been pasted individual letters of the alphabet, a flannel board with cloth letters, or a metal board with magnetic letters, and show them how words can be changed by shifting the letters around. Expose them to computer software programs that teach reading in a logical way (see *Parent-Teacher's Micro-computing Sourcebook for Children*, the most comprehensive list of children's software programs available).

Helping your child learn to read interpersonally.
Reading for these children is a social event. They need to be involved in mutual reading activities. Take turns with them in reading individual words, sentences, pages, or entire stories. Read out loud together. Ask them to teach younger children some words they know. Hold reading parties and invite all the kids in the neighborhood.

Helping your child learn to read intrapersonally. For these youngsters, provide high-interest reading materials, a quiet and cozy reading space in the house, and plenty of time to read leisurely at their own pace, letting them ask you about any words they need help with. They might want to keep a special book of their favorite words for reference in reading and writing stories. They will usually teach themselves to read. High-pressure reading groups at school can easily create reading disability, so make sure they're able to have some quiet reading time there as well.

Exposing children to a "brain-compatible" reading approach may be one of the best things you can give them academically. When they experience the pleasure that comes with success during the first stages of learning to read, they gain positive associations to academic learning that they carry with them for the rest of their lives.

Chasing Away the Times-Tables Blues

Many children find that trying to master the multiplication tables is a frustrating experience. The constant barrage of drills and tests in school leave many children wondering why they have to learn these "stupid" facts in the first place. Children strong in linguistic intelligence often have an easy time memorizing the tables but sometimes don't have a grasp of what multiplication actually means. Youngsters with logical-mathematical gifts may master the concept but have trouble remembering the facts. Children strong in other areas of intelligence may really be in trouble, since the schools generally cater to the linguistically and logical-mathematically inclined. However, *all* children can master both the rote and the reason behind multiplication as long as someone teaches them this skill according to their personal learning style. Here are some ways of reaching children by way of all seven kinds of intelligence.

Multiplication the linguistic way. Since linguistically gifted youngsters learn best by reading, writing, and speaking, use word problems and worksheets from conventional programs, oral drills that enable them to practice reciting the times tables in order, and flash cards that give them an opportunity to orally repeat individual answers. Let them also create their own word problems, either in written form or by speaking them into a tape recorder and then transcribing the text.

Multiplication the logical-mathematical way. Use pebbles, matches, or toothpicks and set up situations where children group them by twos, threes, fours, and so on, letting them discover the principle of multiples through exploratory play. For example, three piles of pebbles with four pebbles in each pile equals twelve pebbles, or $3 \times 4 = 12$. Let them keep charts of their discoveries as an aid in memorizing the facts.

Multiplication the spatial way. Give children a "hundreds" chart—a piece of paper on which are written the numbers 1 to 100 in ten columns horizontally or vertically. Then ask them to color in every second number. This will give them a visual pattern for the 2's. Then give them another hundreds chart and ask them to color in every *third* number for the 3's and so on. Each sheet will provide a different colorful and graphic depiction of that particular multiple, give them both a picture of the concept and a mnemonic aid in memorizing the facts.

Multiplication the kinesthetic way. Have these children walk in a straight line counting out loud with each step, 1, 2, 3, 4, 5, 6 . . . . Then say, "OK, now we're going to clap our hands on every *second* number: 1, **2**, 3, **4**, 5, **6**, 7, **8** . . . ." This can be followed by clapping on every *third* number and so forth. Ask them what they'd like to do besides clapping (possibilities include jumping, skipping, crawling, doing a somersault, or . . .). In this way, they internalize the concept of the multiples in their bodies.

Multiplication the musical way. Select a song that has a natural and even rhythm. Simple folk songs or other songs that are popular with children work well. Then have these children chant, or sing the times tables with them to the rhythm of the song ("2 times 2 is 4, and 2 times 3 is 6, and 2 times 4 is 8 . . ."). If you can't find an appropriate piece of music, use a metronome to keep time. Alternatively, count out loud ("1, **2**, 3, **4**, 5, **6** . . .") singing, shouting, or whispering every second number, every third number, and so on.

Multiplication the interpersonal way. Teach them the basic concept, then ask them to teach it to a friend. Give them some flash cards and suggest that they organize a group flash card competition in the neighborhood. Make a board game out of a manila folder with a winding road drawn in magic marker and times-table problems ($2 \times 3 = ?$) written in on individual squares. Buy some dice and game pieces and invite all the kids in the neighborhood to come and play.

Multiplication the intrapersonal way. Let these children work independently on a group of problems. Provide them with a key for checking their answers, a self-correcting workbook, or a computer software program for learning the times tables on their own. Let them work at their own pace, allowing them to check their answers when they need to, so that they can get immediate feedback on their progress.

How to Teach Anything Seven Different Ways

Once you get the hang of this seven-fold teaching method, you'll be able to teach anything seven different ways. If your child isn't getting it one way, then you have at least six more tries. All it takes is a little creativity and some elbow grease!

Need some more examples? Let's say you want to assist your child in learning the names of the fifty states. Here are seven different ways you can help out:

- **Linguistic**: practice quizzing her orally on the names of the states;
- **Spatial**: get a nice multi-colored map and help her associate the names with the different colors or shapes of the states;
- **Kinesthetic**: find a relief map that she can feel, or a puzzle map that she can take apart and put back together, and assist her in identifying tactile features for each of the states to use in memorizing their names;
- **Logical-mathematical**: help her classify the states into different categories—by first letter, geographical size, population, entry into the union, and so on;
- **Musical**: teach her the different state songs or a song that names all fifty states (if you can't find one, make one up!);
- **Interpersonal**: play a card game such as Concentration where players must match pairs of overturned cards; in this case the name of the state matched with its outline;
- **Intrapersonal**: suggest that she write to the state gov-

ernments of all fifty states (use postcards, they're cheap!) for information she can keep in a scrapbook.

What about homework? If you're lucky, your child's teacher gives your child choices at least some of the time for doing an assignment. Let's say your child comes home with an open-ended homework project to complete for a unit on bird study. Here are seven ways of going about completing the task:

- **Linguistic**: book reports, oral presentations, writing compositions, tape recordings;
- **Spatial**: charts and maps of a bird's migration patterns, pictures of birds;
- **Kinesthetic**: hiking to a bird's natural habitat, building a replica of a bird's nest;
- **Logical-mathematical**: collecting statistics about birds, answering the basic question: "how does a bird fly?";
- **Musical**: finding records or tapes of bird calls and learning to imitate them;
- **Interpersonal**: volunteering in a community project designed to safeguard the welfare of the local bird population;
- **Intrapersonal**: creating a special place of solitude in nature for bird-watching.

Finally, there's that eternal question parents are always asking: "How do I get my child to behave?" Thousands of books have been written on the subject and nobody seems to agree on what to do. Maybe that's because different folks need different strokes. Here are seven strokes for starters:

- **Linguistic**: sit down and have a good chat with your child about why she's misbehaving or ask her to tape record or write down what's bothering her;
- **Logical-mathematical**: reason with your child—show

her the logical consequences of her actions (Rudolf
Dreikurs based an entire discipline system on this approach);

- **Spatial**: tell your child a good, imaginative story illustrating her misbehavior and its possible causes and/or
solutions (for a child who lies, tell "The Boy Who Cried
Wolf");
- **Kinesthetic**: ask your child to act out the misbehavior
and then act out the appropriate behavior and compare
the two;
- **Musical**: find a piece of music that contains the message
you want to drive home to your child or use music as
a relaxing influence for an out-of-control child;
- **Interpersonal**: use group problem-solving activities;
- **Intrapersonal**: use one-on-one counseling, centering
exercises, and lots of patience!

Bridging the Quality Gap in Education

It would be great if every classroom across the
nation used this varied approach to help kids learn. Imagine
what it would be like to walk into any classroom in the
country and see some children clustered around computers,
a few reading by themselves in a corner of the room, several
others busily drawing or modeling with clay, and still others
at work building models or machines. Every child would be
learning in the way that was personally easiest and most
natural.

The reality is that in too many classrooms across America,
students focus on the same boring activities. Even the so-
called individualized programs all too often have children
working on the same mindless exercises in workbooks—
only at different levels. The casualties of this gap between
what education is and what it could be are several million
children mislabeled learning disabled and millions of other
kids who sit in class bored and tuned out, going through the

motions and barely surviving in a system that has little meaning to them.

I sometimes wonder what would happen if we took all the billions of dollars we're pouring into learning disability research, standardized testing, special education, and worthless textbooks and put them instead into enriching the regular classroom—bringing in more equipment, more teachers to provide individual assistance, and more training to help teachers expand their own teaching repertoire. If we did this, millions of so-called learning disabled and underachieving youngsters would lose their disability, and millions of other children would begin to realize more of their true potential in learning. I'm sure of it. Yet I'm also certain that this won't happen overnight—if indeed it ever occurs. What do we do in the meantime? Here are a few suggestions for carrying this approach into your child's school.

Teaching to a Different Intelligence Each Day

Suggest that teachers approach every important skill seven different ways. Naturally, you should also be prepared for their probable reply: "Sounds great! But it's totally impractical in a class of thirty kids." If they tell you this, point out that they don't even have to treat each child differently. Tell them to go on teaching to the whole group if they'd like, but *teach a different way every day.* Suggest that they spend a few extra minutes after the regular reading unit supplementing the traditional program with techniques from this book and other books listed in the resource section. Encourage them to build into the lesson plan activities that make use of the body, the imagination, interaction between students, and music. If they teach to a different type of intelligence every day, at the end of seven days, they'll have given a little something to everybody in the class.

Pointing to Positive Change

Share examples of other schools around the country that teach across the spectrum of abilities. Mention Craddock Elementary School in Aurora, Ohio, where principal Linda Robertson put together a school fair that celebrated learning in all of its colors. This fair included a math arcade, a gymnastics and physical fitness demonstration, an art show, a talent show, and an individual investigations display. Tell them about the Key School in the Indianapolis Public School System, one of the first public schools in the country to apply Howard Gardner's theory of multiple intelligences directly to the curriculum. Suggest that they take a look at the Mead School for Human Development in Byram, Connecticut, where art, music, and dance are integrated with reading, writing, and math in a way that makes use of the latest findings in the neuropsychology of learning. These schools are living evidence that positive change can and does occur in our nation's schools.

Creating Changes in the Classroom

Volunteer to help implement Gardner's seven ways of learning in the classroom. You can take children to a quiet room and use some of the activities suggested in this book. Or you can work with the teacher to create "activity centers" around the classroom that focus on the seven varieties of intelligence: a listening center for musical intelligence, a book nook for linguistic intelligence, a math and science lab for logical-mathematical intelligence, a large open-space area for kinesthetic intelligence, an art center for spatial intelligence, a quiet corner for intrapersonal intelligence, and a round table for interpersonal activities.

Let the battle cry of "seven different ways!" go forth into the schools. Our classrooms have become too one-dimensional. They're stilted by the limited vision of curriculum manufacturers, administrators, and teachers who live in the past. And if the schools resist your battle cry, don't despair. You can still give your child at home what he's not getting at school by following the kind of approach described in this chapter. The next two chapters will help you focus on the two kinds of intelligence that have been most seriously neglected by the schools: spatial and kinesthetic.

CHAPTER 6

Bodywise:
Making Learning Physical

*P*eter was driving his teacher to distraction. Instead of sitting at his desk and concentrating on the lesson, he would get up from his seat and roam at will. His grades plummeted as his teacher's blood pressure rose. Yet one day, Peter's teacher learned an important lesson of her own. Instead of disciplining him, she let him move around the classroom since he didn't appear to be bothering anybody that day. Afterward, she questioned him about the material she'd been teaching and was surprised to discover that he'd absorbed the whole lesson. She began to understand that Peter was a student who needed *to move* in order to learn. She thought of different chores that he could do around the classroom while she taught her lessons, and from that time on, Peter's performance in school began to improve.

In many other classrooms around the country, Peter would have been labeled hyperactive and might have been medicated. Peter's teacher recognized what other parents and teachers around the country are beginning to realize: many children need to learn *through their bodies* in order to make sense out of academic subjects. These *kinesthetic* learners often become frustrated when they have to sit for long periods of time in confining desks doing tasks that involve minimal physical activity. While it may not make sense to let children wander through classrooms like Peter did, there are many practical ways of teaching academic subjects through physical activities. I will describe some of these alternatives later on in the chapter. Before I do, however, let's explore some of the reasons why the body needs to be brought back into children's learning.

Intelligence Begins in the Body

Child development pioneer Arnold Gesell frequently emphasized that "mind manifests itself in everything the body does." Jean Piaget reinforced this when he pointed out that the highest forms of logical intelligence can be traced back to their origins in the body. From the first days of life an infant's body is actively exploring the world and building a preconceptual framework that serves as the root of all later thought. For example, an infant's ability to grasp an object that has been moved away from him demonstrates the capacity to act consistently toward an object despite its changed appearance—in this case, its different location in space. This early capability prepares the way for a later development in middle childhood when children can internally represent objects from a variety of perspectives. They're able to mentally place themselves in the shoes of another person and imagine how an object looks from that point of view. This ability is fundamental to many higher mathematical processes.

In some individuals, thinking retains certain visceral characteristics even at the highest abstract levels. Albert Einstein, for example, spoke of his own thinking process as involving elements "of visual and some of muscular type." William James, considered by many the dean of American psychology, commented on a particular tactile quality to his thought: "I am myself a very poor visualizer, and find that I can seldom call to mind even a single letter of the alphabet in purely retinal terms. I must trace the letter by running my mental eye over its contour in order that the image of it shall leave any distinctness at all." James's "mental fingers" may go back to experiences he had as a young child tracing puzzle pieces or alphabet blocks. In any case, he seemed to have retained this early trait and used it to help him in his creative work (he wrote some of the world's greatest books on modern psychology).

Before humans communicated their ideas through abstract symbols, they used physical movements and gestures. For thousands of years, humanity passed on knowledge from one generation to another through a mixture of chanting, singing, dancing, and drama. Even with the development of written language, this unity of mind and body remained intact for hundreds of years. Dom Jean Leclercq, a Catholic scholar, suggested that monks in the Middle Ages saw reading as a physical activity. He observed that the Latin words *legere* and *lectio* (which, in part, translate as "to read") have a kinesthetic meaning: "When *legere* and *lectio* are used without further explanation, they mean an activity that, like chant and writing, requires the participation of the whole body and the whole mind. Doctors of ancient times used to recommend reading to their patients as a physical exercise on an equal level with walking, running or ball playing." How different this is from our idea of reading today as a mental task based on the "distance senses" of seeing and hearing.

Putting the Body Back into Learning

We seem to have lost this connection between learning and the body in our society. We expect children to sit still in their seats and read, write, or compute silently. Parents and teachers often tell students who fidget while they work to settle down. Sometimes educators refer these kids for testing and they're labeled hyperactive or learning disabled. Sub-vocalizers—or students whose throat muscles quietly work to pronounce the words they read—go to reading specialists who try to help them eliminate this "annoying habit." It's seldom understood that these children could be practicing on some deeper level an oral tradition going back thousands of years. Children who move, speak, and fidget while they work may need to study in this physical way in order to make any meaningful contact with the lifeless symbols in front of them.

We're told that children who need to move while they learn sometimes have neurological problems. The learning disability experts warn us about the "soft signs" of minimal brain dysfunction: mixed dominance—for example being left-handed, right-footed, and right-eyed—difficulty telling left from right, poor eye-hand coordination, certain atypical muscle reflexes, or general clumsiness. Hundreds of tests and programs purport to identify and remediate these "neurological dysfunctions." Yet medical doctors have yet to clearly establish any measurable brain damage in the vast majority of children with these so-called symptoms.

If you have real concerns about your child's sensory-motor functioning at any time, consult with your family physician. However, in general it appears that most of the children showing these characteristics have absolutely no neurological problem. Instead they may have neurological *differences* or unique learning styles—of a kinesthetic and/or spatial kind—causing them to be unbalanced by a system of instruction that splits them off from their natural connection to learning through the body.

Special education programs make the mistake of attempting to isolate children's sensory-motor problems and then train them through artificial activities such as walking on balance beams, crawling on specially designed mats, putting together puzzles, doing mazes, or bouncing on trampolines. If children actually enjoy these activities, that's one thing. However, we've seen in Chapter 4 that research fails to support the effectiveness of most of these activities as learning tools. I would suspect the reason these programs don't work is because children experience life with their whole body, not with the sum of its parts. In order for children to reclaim their bodily processes for learning, they need to be involved in physical activities that are intrinsically worthwhile to them, not isolated from the mainstream of their lives. This goes for each and every child in school, and not simply those suspected of neurological anomalies. The best sensory-motor activities for so-called "special ed" kids are activities that are healthy for all children. These include running, jumping, dancing, hiking, juggling, swimming, martial arts, outdoor games of all kinds, and lots of time to touch, move, and build things with their own hands.

Eliminating Bodily Stresses during Academic Study Periods

Michael Gelb, a bodyworker assisting in British schools, noticed that youngsters experiencing difficulty in schoolwork often tightened up their bodies and restricted their breathing. Teachers added to this tension by pushing harder for answers. Gelb helped these students become aware of their twisted positions and tensed breathing patterns. He encouraged them to open up and expand their breathing and posture. Often this alone would help them see the correct solution or remember the right answer to a particular problem or question.

You can help your child feel more comfortable while studying at home. During her homework time, notice how she sits. Does she appear relaxed and centered or tight and distraught? Ask her to describe the feelings in her body. Then suggest that she experiment with other ways of sitting, or propose that she even try studying in a standing or supine position. Jeffrey Barsch, a California educator, found that his students were able to read and listen better when they were lying down. Each child has her own best way of studying. The strongly kinesthetic child often needs to tap feet or change positions several times in the course of a few minutes. One teacher custom-built a special worktable for such a child that included an old sewing machine foot lever attached to the table leg, so that the youngster could move his foot rhythmically while he studied.

Help your child become aware of her breathing. Is it flowing and easy or shallow and constrained? Sit with her for a few minutes in silence, breathing deep and full breaths at a slow and comfortable pace. This simple act of breathing can unlock the floodgates to natural learning. Georgi Lozanov, a Bulgarian educator regarded as the father of "superlearning," uses breathing as a cornerstone of his teaching method. The learner sits or lies down in a comfortable position, listening to slow and rhythmic musical selections. The teacher reads in a similarly rhythmic manner the words, numbers, or concepts to be learned. The learner breathes deeply in time to the music and words, effortlessly and quickly absorbing information that might otherwise have taken days of hard work to master. For specific information on using this technique, see *Superlearning* by Sheila Ostrander and Lynne Schroeder and *Accelerating Learning: The Use of Suggestion in the Classroom* by Allyn Prichard and Jean Taylor.

Using the Body to Teach Basic Skills

The general picture we get of children in the act of school learning is of them sitting at desks looking up at the blackboard or looking down at their worksheets or textbooks. In this scenario, muscular movement is pretty much restricted to the neck, eye, and hand muscles. For learning to really sink in, however, it also needs to involve complex movements in the large muscles of the arms, legs, and torso.

Body reading. When your child reads at home, have him take little "muscle breaks." These might include jogging, aerobic-type exercises or traditional calesthentics like neck rolls and leg lifts. Any activity that involves the right side of the body making contact with the left side of the body is especially helpful in establishing connections between different parts of the brain. Some of these activities include:

- walking in place exercises where the child alternates touching his right knee with his left hand and vice versa;
- doing sit-ups in which he alternates touching his right knee with his left elbow and vice versa;
- playing Simon Says-type games with instructions like "touch your left toe with your right middle finger" or "touch your right earlobe to your left ankle."

Betty Brenneman, a Wisconsin educator, worked with a ten-year-old boy who'd made little progress in reading during the previous two years. She timed his oral reading before and after doing the kinds of exercises described above and discovered a big improvement in his reading rate and a decrease in the number of errors. Paul Dennison's book *Switching On* includes these and other exercises that can be used during oral and silent reading activities or with any other skill.

When your child meets with an unfamiliar letter or word, suggest that he imagine it to be a miniature playground and invite him to get involved. For example, with the word *put* he could act out crawling through the loop in the *p*, sitting astride the horseshoe *u*, and climbing up the *t* or sliding down its shaft. He can also make the letters with his own body or create entire words with other children and adults.

Give your child opportunities to act out what he reads instead of merely telling you about it. Reading comprehension is frequently a dull activity for kids because they feel no connection to what they're reading. If they put on plays or in other ways dramatize their reading material through pantomime, dramatic recitation, or dance, the meaning will become encoded in their bodies and remain with them for a long time.

Body writing. As mentioned in Chapter 5, bodily-kin-esthetic learners usually do better when they learn to write before they read. This is because writing involves direct interaction between the body and letters, whereas reading as typically taught only uses the distance senses—seeing and hearing. A lot of children get rushed into writing activities requiring the use of only the small motor movements of one hand. These youngsters need to begin their writing experience with large body movements.

Before your child even starts to write symbols he ought to have a lot of experience with freestyle art activities including painting, collage, and working with clay. Then, when he shows an interest in letters and numbers, suggest that he try some of the following alternatives to the usual workbook routine in practicing numbers and letters:

- get huge sheets of butcher paper and write on them in large strokes with thick crayons, magic markers, or a large paint brush;
- go out to the driveway and write on the concrete pavement with sturdy pieces of white or colored chalk;
- go into a dark room and practice "writing" with a flashlight or "light-saber";
- take a squirt gun out to the side of the house and create words in water;
- go out to a muddy field and draw letters and numbers in the mud with a long stick;
- save old toothbrushes and use them as writing implements with finger paints;
- make letter shapes with molded clay;
- practice writing letters or numbers in a sandbox or on a beach.

Supply your child with letters and numbers he can use as models. These should be textured in some way so that he can feel each individual letter shape before writing it. Buy sandpaper letters from an educational supply store or make an alphabet from some of the following materials: sandpaper, bread dough, macaroni, rice, pipe cleaners, yarn, glue, seeds, glitter, clay, cloth, toothpicks, straws, bottle caps, twigs, or wire.

Body spelling. Spelling drills are usually dull affairs for children ("Repeat after me, DOG, *D-O-G*, DOG"). There's no real interaction going on for these youngsters beyond staring blankly at the word to be memorized. To involve the body, suggest that your child perform any of the following activities while spelling a word: jump while saying each letter; alternate standing up and sitting down (*A*(up), *N*(down), *D*(up), AND); alternate jumping and squatting; clap loudly while shouting each letter; lie down on the floor only when repeating the vowels. Ask them to make up their own sequence of body movements.

Body math. An excellent way to learn mathematical concepts kinesthetically is through math manipulatives. These are concrete materials—such as blocks, rods, dice, and chips—that kids actively touch, move, stack, and maneuver to explore relationships at the heart of basic mathematical operations. One commercial brand of math manipulatives, Cuisenaire rods, give children the opportunity to compare and contrast differences in length between several sizes and colors of thin wooden blocks. In playing with the rods, they learn, among many other things, the principle that there are several ways of combining small rods to equal the length of a larger rod. For example, it takes a white rod plus a purple rod to equal the length of a light-yellow rod. A dark-yellow rod plus an orange rod *also* equals the length of a light-yellow rod. This discovery paves the way for a later symbolic understanding that there are several ways of adding numbers together to create the same sum (for example $3 + 3 = 6$; $4 + 2 = 6$; $5 + 1 = 6$). Children experience this principle with their hands first and their minds later.

Manipulatives don't work with all children. Some kids are

turned off to them because schools often use them in the same coercive way they use worksheets. Other kids must go more deeply into kinesthetic learning and rediscover numbers in their bodies. In a sense, they need to explore the meaning of numbers just as they originally developed in the course of history. A measurement such as the foot, for example, was originally based on the length of the king's foot. Our base ten system of place value goes back to the use of ten fingers in counting.

Here are some suggestions for building the body directly into your child's basic math program:

- let your child use her fingers to add, subtract, multiply and divide; teach her chisanbop—a method of mathematical calculation based on the systematic and rapid use of the fingers;
- draw a number line in chalk on the sidewalk or driveway; then have your child practice doing arithmetic problems by walking, running, jumping, or skipping along the number line;
- help your child measure her height and weight, the length of her arms and legs, the area of her skin, and other bodily measurements;
- show her how to use her own body to measure other things—for example, the length of a room in human "feet";
- help her explore different geometric forms through creative body movements;
- assist her in telling time by drawing a large body-sized clock face in chalk on the sidewalk and then have her lie down on it using her arms as the clock's "hands";
- suggest that she act out math word problems instead of simply trying to figure them out in her head.

For other ideas, see the book *Teaching the 3 R's Through Movement Experiences* by Anne G. Gilbert and *Unicorns are Real* by Barbara Meister Vitale.

Kinesthetic Symbol Systems

Consider using kinesthetic symbol systems as alternatives or supplements to the standard English alphabet. Some children experience tremendous difficulty learning to read in spite of creative teaching and may benefit from an alternative symbol system to help them get started. One example of this is the use of braille, a symbol system based almost entirely on the sense of touch. This approach has been successfully used to teach reading skills to children labeled as severe dyslexics. One mother wrote about her fifteen-year-old daughter, Roselyn, labeled everything from mentally retarded to gifted, who still could not read beyond a mid-second-grade level. After ten months of braille instruction, she phoned home from school and excitedly told her mom how she'd passed her tests and completed all the requirements for third grade—a remarkable achievement given her previous school record. Her braille teacher observed that Roselyn's sense of touch was "the most sensitive of any child I have ever taught." This gift appears to be present in other children experiencing reading difficulty. One study observed "retarded readers" showing a significant superiority over "normal readers" on four tests of tactile ability.

Another symbol system involving both kinesthetic and spatial intelligence is sign language. By using gestures and hand signals to create letters, words, and concepts, children who might find reading a chore can experience success. A mother from Alaska wrote me about her daughter, who was having trouble learning to read. She then enrolled with her family in a sign language course at a local college. Her mother wrote: "I wish you could see this 'dyslexic' child learn those signs and recall them with her marvelous memory. She's one of the best in the class." I don't know whether it's coincidence or not, but right about this time her mother reported that she began reading—sat down and read a whole novel in one day. These two success stories are a testimony to the special needs of individuals with strong bodily-kinesthetic intelligence who can succeed when parents and teachers tap this natural channel of learning within them. Even kids who read well may enjoy learning braille or signing as a way of expanding their communication skills.

The Body as an Adjunct to Learning

There are many other ways of bringing the body into learning. At school, simulation, role play, field trips, improvisation, and hands-on activities provide the basis for teaching virtually any subject. One biology teacher had his students learn the rudiments of molecular bonding by assigning to them the roles of atoms. The hydrogen atom could only bond to other student-atoms with one hand, the oxygen atom with two hands. In this way, they learned how different compounds and molecules form. Another teacher taught American history by having students spontaneously act out the roles of newly arrived immigrants from England to colonial America.

At home, you don't have to look far to find areas where kinesthetic learning takes place. Simple chores such as cooking, cleaning, gardening, and helping to fix things around the house develop body-knowing. So do hobbies including carpentry, weaving, knitting, nature study, art activities, and sports of all kinds. In the same way dance, massage, wrestling, skateboarding, karate, juggling, and model-building develop a number of important physical abilities including eye/hand coordination, left-right orientation, balance, reflexes, body awareness, manual dexterity, and all those other psycho-physical skills so important to academic learning. The point is that these activities are worthwhile in and of themselves, and not simply as exercises to "remediate learning dysfunction" or "develop your child's intelligence." Take care not to use them in this way. Children

often resent having adults foist these special "learning activities" on them, and tend to learn best when engaged in
activities for their own sake.

It may seem ridiculous to say this, but children take their
bodies with them wherever they go, whereas they're more
likely to leave their workbooks and folders behind. As more
parents and teachers begin to recognize the importance of
the body in learning, we're likely to see a sharp decline in
the number of so-called disabled learners and a corresponding increase in real learning capacity and enjoyment among
millions of children nationwide. This is also true for the role
of the imagination in learning. The next chapter explores the
importance of fantasy and "visual thinking" in the lives of
children.

CHAPTER 7

The Inner Blackboard: Cultivating the Imagination in Learning

Daydreamer. When parents hear this word used to describe their children in school, they begin to worry. Yet daydreamers may turn out to be highly imaginative children who simply don't have any outlets in the worksheet wasteland for their marvelous powers of fantasy. The schools allow millions of imaginative kids to go unrecognized and let their gifts remain untapped simply because educators focus too much attention on numbers, words, and concepts and not enough on images, pictures, and metaphors. Many of these children may be ending up in learning disability classes and many more may be wasting away in regular classrooms, at least in part because nobody has been able to figure out how to make use of their talents in a school setting. Imagination forms an integral part of every child's development and deserves to be nurtured in practical ways to teach youngsters what they need to learn in school.

Seeing is Conceiving—From Image to Abstract Thought

Growing evidence points to the importance of the mental image as a crucial step along the way toward higher abstract thinking for the young child. As we saw in the last chapter, thinking really begins in the body. However, as the child grows, thinking becomes clothed in the rich fabric of inner imagery. In the first few months of life, problem solving is limited to the body. A baby attempts to get a toy back that has dropped out of sight by swinging his arms to and fro, mimicking the movement that originally led him to acquire the toy. After the first year, however, a child becomes capable of holding an inner image of a lost toy and can use this mental map to help search for it. Many years later, as a teenager, he may rely on purely logical relation-ships as clues to the possible location of a lost possession. Development moves from the body to the image to the concept. Jerome Bruner, George Herbert Mead Professor of Psychology at the New School for Social Research, refers to these three levels of representation as *enactive* (through the body), *iconic* (through the image), and *symbolic* (through the concept). The iconic level is the critical link between purely physical expression and totally conceptual representation. As such, it is really the bridge between body and mind.

While iconic representation may appear developmentally before symbolic knowledge, this doesn't mean that image is inferior to reason. Mental imagery seems to make up the very substance of so-called higher forms of thinking. George Lakoff and Mark Johnson, authors of *Metaphors We Live By*, point out how much of our everyday language is saturated with metaphors having a visual basis; for example, in the world of high finance, commonly used terms include *liquid assets*, *cash flow*, and *hard cash*.

One theorist, Rudolf Arnheim, professor of the psychol-ogy of art at Harvard University, goes so far as to say that *all* thinking—no matter how theoretical—is visual in nature. Even concepts as abstract as "democracy" and "future" have some basis in image, according to Arnheim. The images may not be readily apparent or easily described. However, if one takes the time to reflect, the connection with image will surface. Arnheim cites the case of early twentieth-century psychologist E. B. Titchner, who attended a lecture during which the speaker made frequent and emphatic use of the monosyllable "but." Titchner came to associate the word with "a flashing picture of a bald crown, with a fringe of hair below, and a massive black shoulder, the whole passing swiftly down the visual field, from northwest to southeast." We all appear to carry subliminal visual associations like this one that we associate to commonly used words and concepts.

In a more practical vein, culture owes many of its most advanced scientific and technological discoveries to the workings of fertile imaginations. Nicholas Howe, the creator of the sewing machine, struggled for many months to come up with a workable design for his invention. Finally, one night he had a dream where he was captured by natives who demanded that he finish his invention or die. On his way to the execution, Howe noticed that the spears of the natives had holes near the points. He suddenly awoke with the realization that the needle of his own machine needed to have a hole near the tip. His struggle ended and a new era of sewing convenience began.

Nikola Tesla, inventor of high-frequency-voltage generators, designed machines "in his head" that were precise to the ten-thousandth of an inch. It's said that he could actually test these devices in his mind's eye by mentally running them for weeks, and then examine them for signs of wear. Eugene S. Ferguson, professor of history at the University of Delaware, points out that many objects of daily use—carving knives, chairs, lighting fixtures, and motorcycles—as well as everything from pyramids to cathedrals to rockets, had their design and function determined by technologists using pictorial forms of thinking.

The Flowering and Withering of Imagination in Childhood

Geniuses don't have a monopoly on creative imagination. Most children before the age of seven or eight are highly imaginative. They have the ability to take a simple household object such as a matchbox and transform it into a car, a house, a piece of furniture, an animal, or any of a thousand other objects. They experience dreams vividly, and sometimes wake up feeling uncertain about whether their nighttime adventures have actually occurred or not. They look at smudges on walls and swirling clouds and see marvelous scenes. They spontaneously weave fanciful stories with the skill of a master storyteller.

Unfortunately, this rich imaginative world begins to fade as children enter school—with its demands on imageless thinking, pictureless facts and concepts, and abstract-symbol systems. Imagination has little or no place in schools. Imaginative answers on most tests receive no credit. Teachers discourage fantasy-oriented responses because they take up valuable class time. Budget constraints and the need to cover academic objectives impel administrators to cut back or eliminate entirely subjects such as art and creative writing that allow the imagination to flourish.

Many cases of so-called learning disability that we see now in the country result from this rupture of what should be a natural process of transition from the image to the symbol. Spatially intelligent children who have a flair for imaginative experience enter school and become strangers in a strange land of barren symbols and ciphers. Since no one makes use of their imagination to teach them the skills they need to learn in society, this resource atrophies just as it does in their more successful peers. The potentially creative visionary becomes the bored daydreamer. Fortunately, though, there are ways of bridging this gap between image and symbol and feeding the imagination of all children.

Use Pictures and Images to Introduce Words and Letters

Too many children enter the first-grade classroom with high expectations, only to find a barren world of meaningless symbols on workbook pages, in basal readers, and on the blackboard. Research suggests that most first-graders see the alphabet with the right hemisphere of their brain, where spatial intelligence is generally processed. They see letters as pictures. An *A* is a couple of slanted lines with a horizontal line in the middle or a picture of a tepee or a mountain peak. In later grades, however, children begin to shift their perception of letters over to the auditory-linguistic area of the left hemisphere and learn to regard the letter *A* as an abstract symbol associated with a group of sounds.

Some kids, however, *don't* make this shift. These often tend to be highly imaginative children with strong spatial intelligence. Because they regard letters as pictures, they can't read them as symbols. As a result, they end up with the label dyslexic. What they need is an educational approach that will help them make the transition from image to symbol in a natural way.

Even children who make this shift and learn to read often find reading to be a dull and lifeless activity because the subject was never taught to them in an imaginative way. You can help such children bridge the gap between icon and letter by presenting the alphabet pictorially. To introduce the letter *S,* for example, tell a story about a snake. Let them draw pictures of the snake or make the snake in clay. Finally, draw the snake yourself so that it begins to look more and more like the letter *S.* Point out how the sound a snake makes ("sssssss . . .") is the sound the *S* makes as well. Use your own imagination to create pictures out of the other twenty-five letters of the alphabet. See the book *Alphabatics* by Suse MacDonald for suggestions on how to get started.

Show your child how to draw pictures out of the letters of words to illustrate their meaning. Draw the word *rain,* for example, with little droplets falling off of it, or the word *sun* with an aura of yellow light around it. Write the word *short* squashed down and *tall* in very high letters.

This technique was used with children who were having

a hard time learning to read by conventional methods. Barry was a Florida youngster failing the sixth grade in all subjects except mathematics. Standard remedial techniques resulted in little progress. Finally, educator Barbara Cordoni and her colleagues recognized something that no one else noticed in earlier efforts to teach him: Barry loved to draw. They decided to give him the opportunity to create pictures out of his spelling and vocabulary words. For the word *street* Barry hung lamps from the *t*'s to illustrate a community street scene, drew wheels onto the loops in the word *bike,* and made pictures out of many other words from his schoolwork. During the course of the semester, Barry's grades jumped from "Fs" to "As."

Traced back far enough into the ancient past, the English alphabet was once a picture language or series of ideograms. Several current languages have kept their connections to pictures, including Chinese and the Japanese script known as *Kanji.* In Japan, children learn three different scripts— *Kanji,* and two forms of *Kana,* which is a phonetic system like English. With two basic alphabets to learn, children in Japan have both visual-spatial and auditory-linguistic ways of learning the language. As a result, reading disabilities are rare.

Chinese ideograms have been used as a way of teaching reading to so-called dyslexics in our culture. Some Pennsylvania psychologists took a group of second grade inner-city schoolchildren with severe reading difficulties and taught them to read English material written as thirty different Chinese characters. They wrote: "Children who had failed to master the English alphabet sounds in over one and a half years of schooling immediately understood the basic demands of the task and were able to read sentences in the first 5 or 10 minutes of exposure to Chinese." It appears that these children benefitted from this approach because educators tapped these youngsters' highly developed spatial abilities.

Use Storytelling and Metaphor to Convey Facts and Concepts

Children love to be told stories. Their enthusiasm comes from a very deep place in their psyches, reaching back to ancient times when the history and values of culture were passed on through an oral tradition rooted in imaginative myths and legends. Nowadays, storytelling seems to only happen on Saturday afternoons at the public library, but it continues to be a powerful way to communicate knowledge from one generation to another. In an age when television and technological toys seem to leave little room for the imagination, storytelling provides an opportunity for children to supply their own inner images to match those in the tale. This feeds their powers of visualization.

Storytelling ought to be a regular part of your child's life at home and at school. You can make up your own stories or get them from books. However, don't restrict storytime to reading from books. While this is valuable as a preparation for getting your child interested in reading, kids also love to hear stories told spontaneously. If you rely on books for your source of stories, read the story several times first, becoming thoroughly acquainted with it in your own imagination. Practice telling it out loud in an empty room if you wish. Then tell the story to your child. For more information on storytelling, see the book *Creative Storytelling* by Jack McGuire.

Storytelling is an activity worthy of doing simply for its own sake. However, it also happens to be a great way to teach children academic material. The following illustrates how I use storytelling to teach the concept of multiplication.

The As Much Brothers

Once upon a time there was a man named Mr. As Much who lived alone in the forest. He was walking along one day when he heard a voice crying out in the distance. He hurried to the scene of the voice and came upon a deep hole in the ground. Seeing a man trapped below, he threw down a rope he was carrying and hoisted the man to safety.

The man wept with joy and said, "Thank you! Thank you! I am the good magician in these parts. An evil magician knew I had no magic for getting out of deep holes so he laid this bear trap for me. To thank you, I will foretell your future. You will marry and have three sons. Name your sons Just, Twice, and Thrice. Then when each comes of age, teach them these rhymes. Teach Just the following rhyme, 'Whatever I choose to touch will give me Just as Much.' And whatever he touches will become his. Teach Twice the following rhyme, 'Whatever I choose to touch will give me Twice as Much,' and whatever he touches will double and become his. Teach Thrice, 'Whatever I choose to touch will give me Thrice as Much,' and whatever he touches will triple in quantity."

Sure enough, the man did marry, did have three sons as the magician predicted, and when they came of age he taught them the magic rhymes.

At this point, I usually stop telling the story and ask the children questions like: What would happen if Twice as Much touched two gold coins? (He'd get four gold coins.) What would happen if Thrice as Much touched four diamonds? (He'd own twelve diamonds.) The children draw pictures illustrating the story, on one side of the page showing one of the sons touching something and on the other side showing the result. In this way, they begin to develop images for each of the multiplication facts.

You can use storytelling to teach just about anything. Get your child interested in reading by telling him stories from classic children's literature and having the books available should he ask for them. Make up stories using words from his spelling list. Then have him retell the story in written form, making sure he includes the spelling words. Read his history or social studies textbook and make up stories together that incorporate the places, names, and events described so that they come alive pictorially. Encourage him to create his own stories as a way of making sense out of the material he learns.

Stories often employ metaphor or images that have multiple meanings. Psychologist Robert Samples says that the mind of the child is innately metaphoric and requires an approach to learning that is interdisciplinary, multileveled, and nonlinear. Metaphors, thus, make wonderful seeds to sow in a child's mind. (To use a metaphor!) The possibilities are endless. For example, instead of passing on dull science concepts, create images for these processes. A. C. Harwood, a Waldorf educator, points out that it's senseless to explain the laws involved in the formation of rain to a child in purely scientific terms. "But if you make a picture of God as the great gardener who wishes to water all the fields and plains and forests of the earth, and takes the water from the seas as a man takes water from a well, and lets the water fall so gently that it does not harm even the tenderest flower, and is yet so careful of the water that, when all the plants and creatures have drunk, it all runs pure and sweet back into the sea—if you speak in this manner, the child will see the world in terms he can understand."

The use of metaphor is extremely important in conveying through picture-language ideas that would have no meaning to children in a more rational form. W. J. J. Gordon and Tony Poze, two educators in Massachusetts, have devised an approach to learning they call "synectics," which uses metaphor in teaching a wide range of academic subjects. In American history, they'll ask: "How is the conflict Roger Williams had with the authorities of the Massachusetts Bay Colony like the splitting of an amoeba?" or "If the colonies were the cheese, who is the rat?" In teaching about soil erosion, they'll paint a picture of a "cheerful, happy-go-lucky mountain stream" and ask the child to become this image while telling the story of its journey from the mountains to the sea. If more educators used imagery and metaphor in teaching academic facts and concepts, we'd have a lot fewer "disabled" learners and bored students on our hands.

Inner Visualization as a Key to Memorizing Facts

Many children have highly developed visualization skills that they could use to help learn spelling words, math facts, and other forms of information—if parents and teachers only knew how to show them the way. Studies indicate that up to half of all young children produce *eidetic imagery.* This refers to the ability to experience mental pictures as clearly and vividly as perceptions of external objects. Children with eidetic imagery can look at an object, close their eyes, and scan their mental image for additional details not seen during the original perception of an object. Even children who don't appear to have eidetic imagery skills may be able to develop this capacity. E. R. Jaensch, a pioneer in the field of eidetic imagery, felt that this phenomenon was latent in everyone.

Visualization of this kind can come in very handy during a spelling test. Tell your child that he has an "inner blackboard" in his head on which he can write his weekly spelling list. Tell him to leave the spelling words up on his inner blackboard when the teacher erases the spelling words from the "outer" blackboard. Then, after the spelling test has begun, all he has to do is copy the words from his inner blackboard onto a sheet of paper. It's like having a crib sheet inside of his head! He can use this technique to memorize the times tables, remember history facts, learn vocabulary words, or retain countless other bits and pieces of information.

Educators using neurolinguistic programming (NLP)—an eclectic blend of techniques from neuropsychology, computer technology, and psychotherapy—employ a similar eidetic approach with startling results. One junior high school boy identified as a gifted student was unable to spell and write well. "I was writing words down a hundred times and all I got was writer's cramp. I was in a rut. But the NLP brought me out of it. It gave me a kind of safety net." He now gets A pluses on all his spelling tests. Even kids who are successful in school may find that this method saves them valuable study time or is simply a more natural and easier method of learning.

Visualizing Success in Learning

Some children use their imaginative gifts in a negative way—they hold pictures in their mind's eye of themselves as failures in school. These pictures often come from actual memories of being laughed at by peers or criticized by parents and teachers. Over time, these memories turn into horrific images of humiliation and degradation. These images need to be countered by even more powerful pictures of confidence and self-esteem. The following are some exercises you can use to help your child visualize self-confidence and success.

A Happy Learning Time.
Picture a time when you learned something that was easy and that made you happy inside. Maybe it was learning to ride a bike, paint a picture, play a game, or something else that you do well now. Experience that time all over again. Notice how happy you feel. See how easy it is for you to learn.

The Successful Student.
Picture yourself at school as a successful student. You feel smart. You're confident about learning in every subject. See yourself reading easily and quickly. Notice yourself in class answering all the questions first. Picture yourself taking a test and writing down all the correct answers. The teacher comes by and puts an "A" on your paper. Kids come up to you after class and ask you to help them with their homework. When you go home your parents praise you for doing a great job in school. You feel wonderful for being such a good student!

The Inner Teacher.

Picture a teacher who knows everything. This is your very own "inner teacher." Anytime you have a question about something, you can ask this teacher and get the answer. If you're taking a test and the answer doesn't come to you, ask your inner teacher for the right answer. If you're reading a book and see an unfamiliar word, ask your inner teacher to help you with it. If you're having a hard time understanding a new idea in school, have a conversation with your inner teacher about what is unclear, and your inner teacher will help you understand the idea. Your inner teacher is there just for you, to help you become the best student you can be.

Modify these visualization activities to suit the particular needs of your own child. Allow her imagination free reign. For example, she may create an inner teacher that is an animal, an inanimate object such as a tree, or some other symbolic ally. It's important to honor her individual choice, no matter how far-fetched it may seem. Tape record the exercises so that they can be played back whenever she wants to hear them. Create your own versions of them and engage her in telling her own positive learning fantasies.

Too many children suffer from "imaginitis"—the dulling of the mind by numbers, words, abstract concepts, and social clichés. Ironically, it's the successful students who may suffer most from this condition. Many of these youngsters sacrifice their imaginations to succeed in the worksheet wasteland. We can help these children regain their image-making capacity by building visualization, storytelling, metaphor, and picture-language into our learning methods. When we do this, we're also nurturing their affective development, since inner images often have an emotional charge. The next chapter focuses on emotions, seeing how they can serve either to hinder or to help the learning process that takes place inside your child.

CHAPTER 8

Teaching with Feeling: Opening the Heart to Learning

*E*d burst into the classroom in a fury. He'd just gotten into a fight during recess and couldn't think straight. During class he simmered. He wadded his writing assignment into a little ball and threw it at a classmate. We stopped the lesson and talked about what happened out on the playground. I suggested that he tell me his side of the story—in writing. He spent the rest of the afternoon working on the assignment.

Roger was a physically and emotionally abused youngster. He came into my class and did very little reading. Instead, he worked with clay—making little houses that he lighted up with batteries, wires, and bulbs. He spent hours absorbed in fascination—creating a little village of security for himself that he could never find at home. Almost overnight, he skipped ahead two years in reading achievement.

Sarah entered my special class from a very efficient and competitive classroom where she was overlooked and failing at math. In my class she lined up the puppets in the math corner and began lecturing them sternly. Slowly her own math started to improve.

Each of these childrens' feelings were getting in the way of learning. At the same time, feelings held the key to academic success. Ignored or hidden from sight, they sabotaged these youngsters' efforts to succeed. Acknowledged as real and given an opportunity for appropriate expression, they paved the way for effective learning to occur.

The Inner World of Stress

Many children carry around a deep inner turmoil that remains carefully hidden from view to all but the most trusted of companions. This secret stress has many sources. At home, separation or divorce, sibling rivalry, illness, parent criticism, loneliness or boredom, family financial difficulties, and neighborhood feuds all fuel the stress syndrome. At school, stresses include pressures to conform academically, being humiliated by the teacher or laughed at by students, intense competition in class or during after-school sports, being excluded from group activities, getting low or failing grades, and the threat of violence.

Some children bear their burdens well, and may suffer no clearly observable effects. Other children seem to buckle under the weight of their loads and show visible signs of stress including headaches and stomachaches, restlessness, problems concentrating, irritability, aggressiveness, tight muscles, anxiety, and depression. Many of these youngsters end up in remedial classes or programs for the learning disabled or emotionally disturbed. Many others seem to be outwardly successful in school, yet experience no joy in learning. To help all of these children reach their full academic potential we need to provide them with ways to cope with the stresses in their lives—both the inevitable ones that come up as a natural part of learning and growing, and the sudden crises that require more intensive care.

A key to helping children cope with stress is to understand the role of emotions in their lives. Rudolf Steiner called the years from seven to fourteen "the heart of childhood" because the feeling life—as symbolized here by the heart—predominates over the mind. Every moment of time at this age offers an opportunity for the emotions to be expressed. Sympathy for a wounded pet, laughter at a funny joke, tears after a fight with a friend, and a hundred other emotions come up every day in the life of a child.

Children at this age *need* to experience the poles of feeling—happiness and sadness, hope and fear, jealousy and compassion—in order to have a solid foundation for their later emotional life. A child who's too protected—with only the positive side emphasized—becomes vulnerable to stress when life becomes hard. Yet a child who's exposed to physical or emotional abuse at home, constant doses of violence from exposure to the media, and chronic threat from peers and school becomes burned-out before he's even learned how to cope.

Real learning can't take place in the absence of positive *and* negative emotions. First, there are the old feelings that get stirred up from the past—the fear of starting something new, the humiliation at having tried and failed, the rage toward a world that seems cold in the face of one's own impotence, and the apathy one feels after a string of defeats. But there are also the peak moments—the joy of having conquered what one thought were impossible obstacles, the exhilaration of mastery, and the pride at displaying for others one's newfound skill.

To ignore this complex web of feelings is not simply unwise—it is impossible. Yet this is often what we try to do when helping youngsters at home or school. We attempt to deny their emotional lives and, in so doing, cut them off from the source of energy that connects them to their own natural powers of learning. This compounds the stresses that they have to face. At school, specialists set up behavior modification programs to control emotional expression. Meanwhile, counselors and school psychologists are too busy with testing and administrative paperwork to be of much help to children with emotional needs. At home, parents often are too wrapped up in their own problems to have the time and inclination to sit down and listen to their children. In either place, emotions become intrusions into the lesson plan or homework time instead of motivators that can spur the student on to success in academics.

Children need to have permission to express their joy and

anger freely while learning so that the vitality locked up in these emotions can be transformed into the mental activities associated with academic progress. This doesn't mean that you need to let your kids run roughshod over your life, doing whatever they want. It *does* require, however, that your child's honest expression of emotion in all of its colors be acknowledged, and that your child be given opportunities for channeling his true feelings in a number of positive directions—directions that are detailed later on in this chapter. Let's take a look first, though, at the neuropsychological evidence supporting the central role that the emotions have in learning.

The Feeling Brain: At the Crossroads of the Mind

We tend to think of learning—at least academic learning—as a mental process. Yet recent evidence from the brain sciences suggests that the emotions are vital to higher abstract thinking processes. According to Paul MacLean, director of the Laboratory of Brain Evolution and Behavior at the National Institute of Mental Health in Bethesda, Maryland, we have not one brain but three: a "reptilian" brain, an "emotional" brain, and a "rational" brain. The reptilian brain, consisting of the pons, the medulla oblongata, and a few other structures, controls some of our deepest and most instinctive behaviors, such as territoriality and assertiveness rituals (for example, prancing, preening, and posturing). It expresses itself most directly in the actions of mobs and gangs. The rational brain consists of the two hemispheres referred to as the neocortex. This brain is the source of our highest abstract thinking processes, including the symbolic functions necessary for reading, writing, and arithmetic.

MacLean refers to the emotional brain as the *limbic system,* since it surrounds the reptilian-like brainstem at the base of the skull (limbic means "forming a border around"). It controls many of our emotional responses to the environment, including rage, fear, grief, and joy. Since the limbic system sits right in the center of the brain, it functions as a sort of crossroads for much of what goes on within the central nervous system, uniting emotional impulses in the "lower" brain with rational thought patterns in the "higher" brain. "We have been brought up being told the neocortex does everything," says MacLean in the journal *Science*. "We try to be rational, intellectual, to be wary of our emotions. But the only part of the brain that can tell us what we perceive to be real things is the limbic brain."

Other theorists have come to similar conclusions about the unity of knowing and feeling. Psychiatrist William Gray proposes a model of the mind which says that "ideas are rooted in emotional codes." He calls these codes "feeling-tones." Gray says that these emotional tones are embedded in neuropsychological processes and serve as vehicles through which rational ideas are remembered, associated, and reported. Another way of saying this—in terms of the lives of children—is that youngsters often get more out of the *way* something is being taught than from *what* is being taught or the specific content of the curriculum. If someone teaches a fact to them with anger, enthusiasm, lethargy, or sadness, this stands out much more in the minds of children than the particular facts or ideas contained in the lessons. Some researchers go so far as to say that the human heart may play a key role in central thinking processes. Finally, Jerome Bruner, author of the book *Actual Minds, Possible Worlds*, refers to a colleague of his who suggested that we "perfink" or perceive, feel, and think all at the same time.

Learning problems occur when this unity breaks down. Leslie Hart, an educator and science writer, points out that many so-called learning disabilities actually result when stress causes a child to "downshift" from neocortex or rational functioning to lower brain processes associated with the limbic and reptilian systems. The child who charged angrily into my classroom after a fight couldn't think straight because he was operating primarily under the influence of the lower brain systems. When given a chance to settle down and focus on an assignment that made him think about his feelings, he was able to begin the process of reestablishing those all-important connections between rational and feeling brains.

It's really this balance between feeling and thinking that's most important in the education of the child. Kids are highly sensitive to the world around them. Given the opportunity, they respond to learning materials, ideas, and techniques spontaneously. ('That's bo-ring!" or "Hey, this is fun!") Teaching that disregards the feelings and focuses totally upon the rational mind fails to acknowledge these important undercurrents, seriously damaging any chance for real learning to take place.

I've seen this happen too many times in my own classroom and in scores of classrooms that I've visited. I've observed children working quietly—too quietly—and only appearing to learn. In their obsession with silence, administrators, and many parents as well, might be fooled into thinking that a lot of serious learning is going on in these places. Yet, I'm reminded of what John Goodlad said in his study of 1,000 classrooms: "The emotional tone is neither harsh and punitive nor warm and joyful; it might be described most accurately as flat." Emotionally flat classrooms fail to teach because they neglect the emotional brain.

On the other hand, feelings can also *interfere* with learning. I've seen a lot of learning time wasted in my own classrooms because students' emotions overran the lesson plans. My students brought in so much anger, rage, and humiliation from past learning experiences that these deep feelings constantly blocked pathways to new ideas and skills. In this case, I had a surplus of emotion—too much of that "downshifting" that Hart spoke of above—and needed to focus on building a bridge between the limbic system and the neocortex.

The rest of this chapter focuses on practical activities you can use to make emotions work for you and not against you in your efforts to help your child learn. The first group of ideas tells you what to do when there's too much emotion. The second group of suggestions shows you how to bring the limbic system into academic work that's become too dry and cerebral.

De-Stressing the Learning Environment

When a child's stress levels are too high or the emotional climate is too strong, you need to focus attention on directly relieving stress or working with the actual source of emotional conflict before you can even begin to think about academics.

Centering Activities Reduce Stress

Relaxation techniques help your child feel more at ease. Several ways of releasing tension and centering awareness—including biofeedback, yoga, and meditation—have been used successfully to help lower anxiety levels in children, freeing up emotional reserves for new learning. Stephanie Herzog, a California teacher, spoke at a recent conference about Nick, a second-grader with poor concentration and few reading or math skills. After three months of centering activities, Nick went up to his teacher and said, "Teacher, I really felt it today; I felt the relaxing feeling going down my body." From then on, he was able to focus during the centering time and started to make progress in his academic learning. By third grade he was reading at a fifth grade level and currently is a successful junior high school student.

You don't need to wire up children for biofeedback, turn them into pretzels with yoga, or sit in the lotus position in order to help them unwind. Relaxation experiences can be very simple. Try the following exercises yourself first. Then invite your child to become involved. You might want to modify the exercises to meet your child's individual needs. For each exercise, sit comfortably in a straight-backed chair with eyes closed, feet on the floor, and hands folded in your lap or outstretched on your thighs. Alternatively, lie down flat on a carpeted floor with your hands at your side.

The Balloon:

- Breathe normally for a minute or so, paying attention to each breath you take.
- Now you're a balloon. Take a deep breath and let the air come into you so you get really big. Hold in the air while you count silently to four and then let all the air out.
- Repeat two more times.
- Breathe normally for a minute or two before you get up, noticing the relaxing feeling that's come into your body.

The Body Builder:

- Sit quietly for a minute, focusing on the feelings and sensations in your body.
- Stiffen the muscles of both arms as if you were a body builder flexing his muscles, counting silently to four while you do this. When you reach four, let your arms go totally limp like wet noodles. Repeat this stiffening and releasing routine with your legs, head, neck, back, chest, stomach, and finally with your whole body.
- Remain seated or lying down for two or three minutes before getting up.

My Favorite Place:

- Empty your mind of all thoughts.
- Imagine yourself going to your favorite place, a place where you feel totally safe, happy, and relaxed.
- Spend some time in your favorite place, doing the things you most enjoy doing there. Take as much time as you need.
- When you feel you're ready to come back, imagine yourself returning and feel the contact your body makes with the floor or chair. Slowly begin to open your eyes. Remain seated or lying down for a minute or so before getting up.

Other ways of relaxing include listening to a peaceful musical selection, taking a quiet walk out in nature, or hugging and touching. Your child may want to engage in his own activities, including spending time with pets, being with friends, getting involved in sports, or playing a favorite game. All of these experiences help to promote relaxation if they're done in a gentle and noncoercive way.

Tranforming Feelings Through Art

Create opportunities for expression through art, music, dramatic play, or physical movement. The arts channel bothersome feelings into constructive pathways, helping to reduce overall stress levels. Children who show their anger or fear in red and black paint, by noisily banging on a drum, or through jumping up and down in rhythm to a musical piece, drain off excess emotion that may have clogged up their own learning arteries. Artistic expression opens the heart to new learning, allowing children to gain control over their feelings and letting them transform strong emotions into new and creative energies.

Provide your child with materials for artistic expression: paint, clay, or collage supplies for visual art; simple and sturdy musical instruments for rhythmic expression; puppets for dramatic play; or music and space for creative movement. Offer a few basic rules about the use of the materials and let your child do the rest. See *Leap to the Sun* by Judith Peck and *Windows to Our Children* by Violet Oaklander for other ideas on bringing out emotional expression in safe and therapeutic ways.

Easing Your Child's Load at Home and School

Help remove some of the daily stress factors that get in the way of effective learning for your child. Sometimes youngsters are saddled with too much responsibility—care of younger siblings, household chores, extracurricular activities, homework—and they get stressed out from the load. Stress' wear and tear on children may show up in learning performance before it begins to affect physical health. You can help by lightening the load where possible and encouraging your child's teacher to do the same. Ask your child which extracurricular activities he'd like to eliminate so that he can have more time for free play. Perhaps homework assignments might be reduced or modified to reflect his current interests. Finally, since change is associated with stress on many levels, try to regulate your family's daily routine with consistent meal and sleep schedules, minimizing abrupt shifts in the rhythm of your child's life.

Providing Self-Help Skills to Combat Stress

Talk with your child about the emotional conflicts that may be at the heart of a learning problem. It seems that with all the recent attention given to the learning disability theory, we've forgotten about emotional blocks to learning. Jack Canfield, a leader in the field of self-esteem education, once told me about a fourth grade child who was still experiencing problems in learning how to read. Working with the child individually, Jack asked the child to close his eyes and report on what he experienced. The child said that he heard his second grade teacher yelling at him and telling him how he'd never amount to anything in life. Jack had the child speak to this imaginary teacher, pouring out the rage he felt at being humiliated in this way and affirming his own ability to succeed. This experience was enough to help move the child past his reading frustration toward school success.

You may be able to accomplish similar results simply by sitting down with your child in a nonthreatening atmosphere and talking with her about a teacher, a low grade, a troubling paper, or a bothersome classmate. Ask her to identify the problem, the feelings that come up for her around that problem, and finally a possible solution. In being a facilitator rather than a judge or arbitrator, you can help your child come up with answers to her own problems, and provide her with important self-help skills in coping with stress.

Getting Expert Help When You Need It

Professional counseling may be necessary to help your child cope with acute stress factors. Sometimes the problems a child confronts are too emotionally charged or deeply rooted to be easily dealt with in face-to-face conversations between parent and child. Physical abuse, the death of a parent or sibling, personal illness, divorce, or severe inner turmoil of unclear origin may call for the presence of a trained counselor, psychologist, or psychiatrist. Make sure in such a case that you work with a licensed professional who has specific training and experience in your child's particular area of difficulty. But that doesn't mean you should turn complete responsibility for helping your child over to the experts. Work cooperatively with your counselor to develop self-help skills you can use to assist your child at home. *The Child in Crisis* by Patricia Doyle and David Behrens gives specific suggestions for helping your child cope with these acute life stresses.

From Rage to Reading: Learning the Emotive Way

Once children's emotional lives settle down to the point where they don't overwhelm the learning environment, it's time to begin using that affective voltage to charge their learning batteries. This isn't always easy to do in the beginning—it's a little like trying to catch a stampeding elephant with a butterfly net. Yet there are many techniques for motivating a stressed-out learner that are vastly superior to Ritalin, behavior modification, or plain old-fashioned shouting. These methods work because they transform raw, unbridled emotional energy into productive academic activity.

Use Writing and Drawing to Release Emotion

If your child is angry or in conflict, get her to write about or draw the experience. The Italian psychiatrist Roberto Assagioli said that writing is a wonderful catharsis. He recommended writing nasty letters to people you are angry with, and then not mailing them. You can use this approach with a child who is mad at a parent, peer, or teacher. At times like these you must be especially tolerant and allow free expression, both in what words are to be used and in the final appearance of the writing. By letting her discharge emotion in this way, you're helping her transform rage into reason.

Use Creative Writing as a Means of Emotional Expression.   New York poet Kenneth Koch successfully used this approach with stressed-out children in urban school systems. He discovered these kids could easily speak about the problems in their lives when they used the fluid medium of unstructured poetry as a means of expression. Letting young people talk in simple unrhymed patterns about their own inner worlds gives them the opportunity to bridge the gap between verve and vowel. Here, for example, is a short poem written by a student in one of my own classes who was coping with a number of anxiety-provoking stresses in his life:

Spiders are ugly. They live in your mouth. They are very scary. And they drink your blood. And they crawl in your ear.

Koch's book *Wishes, Lies and Dreams* as well as the very fine *Whole Word Catalogue* produced by the Teachers and Writers Collaborative in New York City, provide many wonderful ideas and themes for children to use as starters in expressing their inner lives.

Reading with Feeling

Let your child build a reading vocabulary from words that have an emotional charge.   Sylvia Ashton-Warner called this method "organic reading" and wrote about it in her acclaimed book *Teacher*. Every day, ask your child for a word that she would like to learn how to read. Print each word on a 3" × 5" index card and let her keep the completed cards in a recipe box or use a spiral notebook where all the words beginning with *A* are kept on the first page, all the *B* words on the second page, and so on. Don't worry about whether the words are too difficult. Since they come from her own interest and experience, they are probably surcharged with Gray's "feeling-tones" and are likely to be remembered. Kids in Ashton-Warner's classroom came up with words like *ghost, kiss, daddy,* and *kill.* After your child accumulates several words, help her build sentences and stories from her collection. She can write down these stories in a homemade book and illustrate them with colored pencils, crayons, or paints.

Choose reading materials that stimulate emotional responses. Psychoanalyst Bruno Bettelheim and educator Karen Zelan point out in *Learning to Read: The Child's Fascination with Reading* that a major contributor to reading failure in our schools is the sheer banality of the reading material to which most children are exposed. Children are emotional beings and often can only be reached by books that have an affective charge or that acknowledge their feeling lives in some real way. For those youngsters who are having trouble learning the code, simply written books on affective themes may serve to unite the lower and higher brains. Books such as *Where the Wild Things Are* by Maurice Sendak and *There's a Nightmare in My Closet* by Mercer Mayer speak to the dark side of a child's inner life, but in a way that's made safe for them. *The Temper Tantrum Book* by Edna Preston and *I Was So Mad!* by Norma Simon acknowledge anger as an important part of the child's life. *Helping Children Cope: Mastering Stress Through Books and Stories* by Joan Fassler is a wonderful guide for parents in choosing literature for children dealing with specific emotional traumas such as divorce, illness, or death. Children themselves will tell you through their own enthusiasm which books have meaning for them and which books leave them flat. Pay attention to those responses. Properly nurtured, a child's early excitement about books will pave the way for a lifetime of enjoyment in reading.

Choosing to Learn

Children often find themselves in situations where they have little or no control over what they learn. No one pays attention to what *they* feel about their educational lives. Teachers evaluate them, determine what their needs are, and give them teaching materials and techniques that will supposedly help them learn. The children have little input into this process and even less once the program has begun. They receive workbooks and assignments to complete, texts to read, and tasks to perform—but nobody seems to notice the feelings aroused within them from this whole dehumanizing process.

Such neglect of children's emotional worlds leads to inner frustration and effectively blocks learning. If they become apathetic, then they might quietly fade away into a corner of the classroom where they may continue to stagnate until high school graduation. Perhaps they will join the million or so students annually who leave school functionally illiterate. If they respond with rage and anger, then they could end up with the label "emotionally disturbed" or "behaviorally disordered" and have an entirely new program drawn up for them, again without opportunities for negotiation.

Children have a right to participate in choosing the kinds of materials, techniques, and approaches to be used in their educational careers. Because they've lived with their personal learning styles all their lives, they are usually the best ones to talk with about how they learn best. It's only reasonable that their own feelings be taken into consideration during the process of developing an educational program.

Involving Children in Educational Planning

Allow your child to be present during school meetings, parent conferences, and informal discussions that involve

her educational future. Insist on it, even if the teacher resists. Let your child know she can make suggestions, give input, and have an important say in the planning of her educational future. Don't merely give lip service to this offer but practice it all the way down the line. I've participated in too many conferences where children were ushered into a tense meeting-room atmosphere only to be offered a token opportunity to speak. I never saw a child say a single meaningful thing that reflected an inner belief or emotion in this context. Yet in a one-to-one relationship or in a small, informal group where there was trust and positive regard for the child, this same youngster would make it very clear what her feelings were about being moved from one classroom to another or about some other educational change.

Give your child choices in the setting up of any learning experience. Consult her as much as possible concerning what is to be learned, the way in which a requirement is to be met, and the kinds of materials to be used for any learning activity. I found children's reading performance to be far better when I gave them a choice in what they read to me than if I simply assigned them a book. At home, allow your child to set her own time and place for doing homework and encourage her teacher to provide options in the assignments he gives.

These suggestions are a beginning in allowing emotions to take a central place in your child's learning. However, they can't replace the single, most important factor in her emotional well-being, and that's your own relationship to her. We'll explore that topic in the next chapter.

CHAPTER 9

The Learning Network: Building Support Systems in Your Child's Academic Life

"*H*aven't you done your homework yet?" "Do you call that mass of scribbles a book report?" "Hey dummy, when are you going to shape up and be like the rest of us?" Many children find their learning relationships to be sadly lacking in positive strokes. At home, parents nag them about low grades, poor study habits, or uncooperative be-.tavior. At school, teachers criticize them for illegible assignments, not following directions, or having a poor attitude. On the playground, peers taunt them for not following the crowd, being in special programs, or saying and doing things in a different way. Their learning network sags in the middle. It fails to give them the encouragement they need in order to feel like competent, successful human beings. As a result, they tend to stay locked in a pattern of learning failure—or in the case of achieving students, "learning doldrums"—rather than discovering the truth of their own personal learning style.

No child learns in a vacuum. Beginning in infancy, a baby's efforts to master the environment are mediated by those around him. Grasping for a toy, the infant finds his performance ideally facilitated by encouraging family members who help to arrange the situation so that it is neither too easy nor too difficult for him to attain his goal. On the other hand, an infant who is told harshly not to touch, is given the toy without expending any effort, or is surrounded by anxious onlookers, never experiences the joy that comes from having his own efforts rewarded. These patterns get laid down early in life so that by the time the child enters school, he finds himself involved in a complex series of mutual interactions with the world that either carry him into school with confidence or cause him to doubt his own self-worth.

Many children all too often fall onto the negative side of the learning ledger. Living in a world where people regard their uniqueness as unacceptable, they either quietly submit and spend much of their lives attempting to be as bland and normal as possible, or they go on the defensive and end up in a perpetual battle with those who might otherwise help them learn.

What children need, beginning in early life, is a trusted ally; someone who believes in them and supports the way in which they learn best. They need an ongoing relationship with at least one competent adult who can serve as an advocate for them in the world. This positive learning relationship can then be a model for how other interactions in their lives might take place. Even in the midst of a choppy sea of criticism and contempt, this relationship can serve as a bright beacon that guides them toward constructive learning later on in life.

If you're a parent, you're in a good position to take on the role of trusted ally in the world of learning. Spending more time with your child than anybody else, you have the best chance of discovering and effectively working with the bright spots in his educational life. Teachers have their hands full with many other children, making it difficult for them to provide the closeness that this special relationship requires. Moreover, children often end up seeing several teachers a day so that they don't have the opportunity to form a close bond with any one adult in school. The rest of this chapter will focus on ways in which you can use your relationship with your child to improve academic learning and to create a setting for success in his life. Teachers, therapists, or friends of children can also apply these principles to their relationships with the children in their lives.

Symbiotic Learning: How You and Your Child Can Teach Each Other

Any real learning experience you engage in with your child benefits both of you. While it's clear that adults transmit culture to the younger generation, adults have a lot to gain from children as well. King Solomon said: "None is so great that he needs no help, and none is so small that he cannot give it." When you engage in a learning experience with your child, you have the opportunity to gain insight into how *you* learn, and you may be surprised by how much your child can teach you.

It's important to recognize this creative symbiosis. If you feel you have nothing personally to gain from helping your child, you'll be less inclined to put yourself entirely into the learning process. On the other hand, if you see yourself as the "all knowing" teacher, you may find your child resenting this attitude and closing off possibilities for further learning. A balance is needed, so that you can open yourself up to new experiences as a learner, and at the same time, feel the joy that comes from teaching your child something new.

Make Homework Time a Mutually Enjoyable Experience

Many parents tell me that they've given up helping their kids with homework because every time they try, the kitchen table turns into a battlefield. Doing homework together can be one of the best ways to create a positive learning bond with your child. These sessions often go wrong because they're perceived by parents and children alike as power struggles. Parents may be overly critical of their children's mistakes and lead them to make even more errors. Children may get frustrated, angry, or bored—and stimulate these same emotions in parents. If parent-child study time is to succeed it needs to be, above all, a positive and cooperative endeavor voluntarily undertaken by both sides. Here are some pointers for making it a success:

Let your child set the agenda for the study session. Some kids like to start at the beginning of an assignment and work sequentially through each problem or step of an assignment until reaching the end. Other children begin with the easiest part of the assignment and move toward the hardest sections (or avoid them altogether!). Still others use nonlinear methods for getting homework done. It's important to honor each child's personal strategy for studying, since this approach comes from personal choice and is likely to be backed up with enough motivation to get the job done.

If your child has trouble knowing where to start, you can guide him by asking "What do you need the most help with now?" Focus on one problem or step at a time. If your child has forty difficult problems to do, select a representative sample and work on it together. Ask him to verbalize what is confusing, difficult, or unclear. Listen carefully, acknowledge the difficulty, and respond clearly in a way that helps.

Avoid using rewards and punishments. Bribing kids with privileges and prizes communicates the message to them that learning is not worth pursuing in its own right. Punishment is even worse since it causes your child to associate learning with pain. Use verbal praise as a reinforcement only when you genuinely feel it. Praise should be a natural outcome of your own excitement and joy at seeing your child do well.

Give clear, nonjudgmental feedback. If your child is having problems with a subject, he's likely to be hypersensitive to criticism in that area. So don't say: "You mean you still don't know how to borrow?" but suggest instead "I see that borrowing is difficult for you." Focus on specifics in giving feedback (not "You're wrong," but "I noticed you added 2 and 2 and got 5)." Ask him to describe the steps he went through to get a particular answer. In this way, he can often learn to give himself feedback and use important self-correcting strategies in his schoolwork.

If you don't know how to help with a particular problem or skill, be honest and say so. Sometimes parents would rather bluff their way through children's questions or assignments rather than admit ignorance. Yet your child will usually suspect this and may benefit more from your own honesty than anything else during the homework session, since this shows him that it's okay not to know something. Together you can go to a third source—a spouse, a friend, a textbook, or a teacher—and discover the answer.

Avoid power struggles. Your child may begin to feel pressured, judged, or smothered by your attempts to help, and actively resist these efforts with any number of ingenious manipulations, including whining, refusal to work, changing the subject, leaving the room, arguing, and intentional mistakes. These are your child's attempts to experience a sense of control in a situation that makes him feel helpless. Whenever you begin to feel as if the session is turning into a power struggle, you can take a deep breath, say the word *relax* silently, and ask him if he would like to continue. (You may want to use some of the relaxation exercises suggested in the last chapter as an aid in de-stressing the atmosphere.)

Beyond Homework: Learning Together in Real Life

Don't limit your learning times together to homework sessions. Learning occurs all the time in the hundreds of interactions that take place between you and your child every day. Remember that he learned one of the

118 ◄§ IN THEIR OWN WAY

most complex skills in the world—the English language—
just by listening to you and your friends speak and practicing the patterns he heard. There are many activities you can
share with him that will naturally provide rich opportunities
for academic growth. Games, for example, are excellent
learning tools. Word games such as Scrabble and Anagrams
teach spelling and vocabulary skills. Strategy games including chess, checkers, Go, and many card games stimulate
logical problem-solving capabilities. Games like Monopoly
offer opportunities for arithmetic computation. Other activities such as cooking, carpentry, gardening, shopping, and
animal care provide the basis for learning hundreds of skills
and competencies.

It's important to keep in mind, however, that these activities should be engaged in for their own sake—because
they're intrinsically worthwhile—and not because they
teach specific academic objectives. Pressuring kids to learn
in this way, or even pointing out to them in the course of
an activity that they are learning something may sour them
to future experiences of this kind. Trust that these activities
help your child learn, and focus your energies on seeing to
it that he is engaged and excited, not on whether he's getting
the skill or objective you want him to learn.

Practice What You Teach

You influence your child's learning on many
different levels—seen and unseen. On an unconscious level,
you transmit your own values and attitudes about learning.
If you had negative school experiences of your own, then
your child all too easily absorbs these feelings. That's why
it's especially important for you to work on developing your
own deep love of learning. *It's the single most important thing you
can do to help him academically.* If you worry about his reading
progress yet rarely pick up a book, then what kind of example are you providing for him? On the other hand, if you

actively practice the skills you want him to learn, then you provide an example he can emulate. A Wisconsin mother writes about how she made this principle work for her in helping her children with their homework:

> I noticed recently that when I was helping my kids with their reading that I sometimes found myself getting up and doing household chores, in which case I did not hear their requests for help or I would try to put them off until I was finished with what I was doing. On the other hand, if I sat right by them and watched what they were doing, I found myself jumping to explain things that they could surely have figured out and worse yet, becoming bossy and impatient. Quite by accident I found the perfect solution one day when I was engrossed in a novel that I couldn't put down and they wanted help with their work books. I just sat close at hand and continued reading. I was right there and available when they wanted help, but not so bored that I was sticking my nose into their business all the time. Best of all, there I was actively enjoying the very skill that they were working to master. Now I really look forward to sitting down with them to work on reading.

This is the way most knowledge was transmitted from generation to generation until very recently. A child would learn a skill by being in the presence of a competent adult who actively practiced that skill, whether it was hunting, fishing, carpentry, printing, sewing, cooking, reading, or writing. It's only recently that culture appointed a number of "specialists"—called teachers—to pass on its most important skills. Jim Trelease, author of *The Read Aloud Handbook,* suggests that children learn to read, not from reading drills and phonics worksheets in classrooms, but from sitting in the lap of a trusted adult and listening to stories from early childhood on. This method works because parents model the behavior that they want their children to learn in a comfortable and relaxed setting—the home.

The parent's workplace is also an excellent "classroom" to show children new possibilities and teach them new skills—

other times it's a parent's hobby, a sport, or a volunteer activity in the community. Children will often pick up a great deal simply through observation and imitation. More importantly, they're seeing parents doing what they love to do. It's that zest for learning which ultimately impresses children the most and becomes part of their own belief system about learning and growing.

Allow your child to see you in the act of learning something new, whether it's figuring out the instructions from a do-it-yourself kit, trying a new cooking recipe, or learning a dance step. Don't be afraid to show your own inadequacies. Letting him see an adult who can face challenge without giving in to frustration provides him with something he can refer to during his own difficult times in learning.

Don't overlook the possibility of bringing in members of the community to help your child learn something that you don't know how to do. Apprenticeships used to be the primary method of education for teenagers and young adults. Nowadays, many kids are wasting away in school when they could be actively learning a skill or trade in the community that might net them a hefty income. If your child is interested in fixing things, see if he can't spend some time every week at a mechanic's shop. If he likes to cook, give him a chance to work in a restaurant. If his interest is animals, see if there's a veterinarian in town that could take him under his wing and offer some small jobs around the clinic. Start looking at the members of your community as a valuable resource and make their expertise a part of his learning network.

Working Together with Your Child's Teachers

If your child sticks out in any way from the norm, then the chances are that at one time or another there's been friction at school between teacher and child.

Unfortunately, as we've observed throughout this book, many teachers expect all children to learn in roughly the same way, with little allowance for diversity in learning styles. A child who requires a different approach may prove to be quite an irritant. If he is in a special education classroom, the teacher is often more sensitive to individual differences. However, in these settings the teacher may tend to view him as handicapped or disabled rather than as a child with a unique learning style. Consequently, you need to be resourceful in either setting and come up with strategies to help smooth out the relationship between him and his teacher.

When school difficulties arise, arrange for a meeting with his teacher to talk about constructive solutions to the problem. Include him in the discussions, attempting to smooth out any communication breakdowns that may fuel the problem. Perhaps the teacher has a strong linguistic intellect while your child is more bodily-kinesthetic. In such a case, you may need to diplomatically suggest ways in which his needs for movement and touch can be satisfied in the classroom through specific learning activities. It could be that he holds a grudge against the teacher for being unfair on a test, or withholding privileges for misbehavior. In this case, you may need to help him express these feelings to the teacher so that the teacher can clarify test items or more clearly communicate class rules for appropriate conduct.

Avoid creating an adversarial relationship with the teacher that can only subvert your efforts to improve the relationship between teacher and child. Teachers are wary of overbearing parents and may resent what they perceive as any pushiness on your part. Yet at the same time, serve as a strong advocate for him, and be wary of attempts to mystify with educational jargon or unclear judgments. Don't accept "Your child has auditory discrimination problems" when the teacher really means "Ed doesn't like listening to my reading lessons." Help your child communicate his own needs for learning directly to the teacher—books he would

like to read in class, subjects he would like to study, projects
he would like to do. If, after your best efforts to work out
communication snags, there is still a residue of negativity
between teacher and student, then consider some of the
alternatives listed in Chapter 4 for schooling your child elsewhere.

Learning among Friends:
The Power of Peer Teaching

Nineteenth-century British educator Joseph
Lancaster once taught more than 1,000 children at a time
using children to teach small groups of other children.
Young people seem to have an uncanny knack for tuning
into the needs of their peers. They tend to avoid some of the
pitfalls that you may encounter with your child, including
his feeling inferior to a powerful adult. At school, encourage
your child's teacher to use peer-led reading groups, study
sessions, and games involving lots of social interaction.

Ironically, children may not grasp a new idea or skill until
they have a chance to teach it to somebody else. A Georgia
mother comments:

> I have noticed that "LD" children have a more complex system
> for understanding than "normal" kids do. For example, my 13
> year old daughter, Louise ("LD") was unable to understand the
> concept of borrowing in subtraction or carrying in addition—no
> matter how many different ways I tried to demonstrate it to her.
> I finally gave up. I started to teach her 8 year old sister Patsy
> ("normal") the same concepts. She was learning well, but still
> a bit confused. Louise took over and was able to show Patsy
> clearly how it was done. Only then, while teaching, did it make
> sense to her.

Learning while teaching others may be particularly effective
for children with strengths in interpersonal intelligence. If

there are younger siblings or neighborhood tots about, you might suggest to your child that he teach them a simple skill. This not only clarifies his own thinking but gives him the opportunity to experience learning success with another person.

By now you should have a sense of the important contribution that social interaction makes to your child's academic performance. Your own attitudes toward learning and the time that you spend with your child in learning activities may have a greater impact on his academic success than all of his teachers combined. All it really takes from you is a simple expression of interest, some positive times together, and a genuine effort to bring others into his learning life in a constructive way. Beyond this aim is an even subtler factor—the positive expectations that you have for your child's success. It's to this "hidden factor" in learning that we now turn in the next chapter.

CHAPTER 10

Great Expectations: Creating Positive Beliefs in Your Child and Yourself

*G*oethe once said, "Treat people as if they were what they ought to be and you help them to become what they are capable of being." This attitude is sadly lacking in much of our educational work with children. Children need megadoses of positive experience in learning. They need to be surrounded by people who see the best in them. Instead, many children learn to conform to the limits that parents and teachers subtly place on them. This chapter will explore the tremendous impact that your expectations—both positive and negative—have on your child's learning progress and potential. While expectation is an invisible phenomenon, it represents a potent influence on your child's educational career, so read this chapter especially carefully.

School Labels: Let the Buyer Beware

It can begin almost imperceptibly. A parent reads a book about learning disabilities, underachievement, or emotional problems in children and answers the questions these books invariably ask: "Is your child a discipline problem?" "Does he reverse letters?" "Did your child have trouble learning to crawl?" This gets the parent thinking, "Oh yes, I remember a time when Johnny had that problem." A syndrome begins to emerge out of previously dislocated bits and pieces of information. Suddenly, Johnny has a label.

We now know that the expectations adults have for a child's learning capacity can greatly influence scholastic performance. Harvard psychologist Robert Rosenthal demonstrated what he called the *Pygmalion effect* in a series of remarkable experiments several years ago. Rosenthal and his colleagues went into a public school district at the beginning of the academic year and tested children using, among other tests, an obscure measure of intelligence. After scoring the results, Rosenthal presented teachers with a list of students in their classes who promised to be "late bloomers" based upon their performance on that particular test.

In truth, this test had absolutely no validity at all and the list of favored children had been picked at random from the whole group. At the end of the year, Rosenthal tested all the students on several measures of achievement and intelligence and discovered that the late bloomers made greater gains than any of the other kids in class. He hypothesized, on the basis of these results, that the teachers' expectations caused the so-called late bloomers to progress as much as they did. The teachers seemed to expect more from these kids, and they got it.

Unfortunately, the Pygmalion effect works in reverse as well. In one experiment, two groups of elementary school teachers were shown a videotape recording of a fourth grade boy engaged in different activities. Before the showing, one group was told that the child was normal while experimenters informed the other group that he was learning disabled. After the presentation, both groups filled out referral forms for the boy. The group informed that the child was learning disabled rated him more negatively than the control group.

Another study showed that when first grade teachers perceive a child to be "at risk" for learning and behavior problems, they are three times as likely to criticize the child in class. Constantly criticized children don't learn as well as those who receive a balance of praise and constructive criticism. Teachers don't expect as much from "disabled" learners, don't challenge them as much as "normal" children, and don't provide them with the positive attention they need to thrive as successful students.

It's no wonder, then, that self-concept scores of children labeled learning disabled tend to be consistently lower than those of nonlabeled kids. The belief "I am a disabled learner" may limit a child's learning potential far more than whatever was causing the original learning difficulty. Psychologists are now identifying a new phenomenon in these youngsters called *learned helplessness.* These children believe that their own efforts to learn will inevitably result in failure. When they succeed, they tend to attribute their triumphs to luck—something outside themselves. When they fail, they tend to blame themselves and their own lack of ability. After a while they just stop trying. And the label provides them with another reason to fail.

All children—not just those labeled learning disabled or underachievers—are sensitive to negative suggestions from parents and teachers. In a sense, the subliminal expectations that parents and teachers silently implant in children represent a very subtle form of hypnotic induction. Former Stanford professor Ernest Hilgard observed that children between the ages of seven and fourteen are highly susceptible to hypnotic suggestion. Thus, at the age of greatest vulnerability, kids are most likely to receive negative messages about their learning abilities and school performance. What this means is that our children are being brainwashed into thinking about themselves as poor learners before they even have a chance to reach adulthood and think things through for themselves.

Attributions such as "Suzy's lazy" or "Melvin just doesn't measure up to his father" eat away at these kids' self-esteem, sabotaging their learning potential and turning them into cynical or closed off students. Psychoanalyst Erik Erikson characterized the elementary school years as a struggle between the forces of industry in the child ("What I produce is really worth something") and inferiority ("Whatever I do is no good"). Children who move through their school careers having to listen to parents and teachers subtly tear them down or measure them up against an impossible standard, face the prospect of emerging from this important developmental period with a conception of themselves as inferior people.

The Alchemy of Expectation

Parents and teachers *can* change their current expectations so that children really learn to believe in themselves as competent learners. Like the alchemists of old who specialized in turning lead into gold, you can transform your own invisible beliefs about your child—beliefs that may be dragging him down academically or personally—into high, yet realistic, expectations for learning success. The rest of this chapter will explore concrete ways that you can do this.

Viewing Learning Behaviors as Positive Traits

Stop using negatives in describing children and their learning behaviors. Some might think this is impossible to do with children, but in truth, most so-called symptoms of learning difficulty can be reframed into positive developmental signs of growth. If you don't think so, take a look at Table 6–1, which matches common negative traits of children to those same traits viewed in a more positive way. You might be thinking that these "golden" terms are nothing but euphemisms for describing some clearly troubled or troublesome children. Yet we've seen from studies of teacher-child interactions how the terms we choose to focus on can make a crucial difference in a child's growth and learning.

Table 6–1: Turning Lead into Gold

Lead	**Gold**
A child who's judged to be:	*Can also be considered:*
learning disabled	learning different
hyperactive	a kinesthetic learner
dyslexic	a spatial learner
aggressive	assertive
plodding	thorough
lazy	relaxed
immature	late blooming
phobic	cautious
scattered	divergent
daydreaming	imaginative
irritable	sensitive
perseverative	persistent

Discovering Skills and Interests

Instead of dwelling on the problems your child is having at school, try to discover his talents and abilities. I tell parents and teachers to become "strength detectives" and locate as many talents and abilities as they can. This isn't easy to do because there are so many books out on the market giving us "warning signs" and so many tests available to find out what's wrong with people, that we just haven't had enough practice doing this. Here's a simple series of questions you can ask in guiding your own discovery of your child's abilities.

Acquired skills. What does your child already know how to do? Ask your child's teacher what skills he already possesses, what he gets the highest test scores in, and what learning competencies he's displayed. If the teacher doesn't know, find another classroom for your child.

Personal interests. What excites your child? Look around the house and notice what kinds of hobbies he has, what kinds of games and toys he plays with, what T.V. programs and movies he enjoys, and what sorts of books or pictures he likes.

Special talents. What actual or potential talents does your child have? Use Howard Gardner's model of multiple intelligences as a guideline. Remember, a talent may not be something that has yet developed, but be on the lookout for any sign of its budding. Yehudi Menuhin loved the sounds of the San Francisco Symphony Orchestra as a three year old and asked his parents for a violin and violin lessons for his fourth birthday. They gave him both. Albert Einstein traced his interest in physics back to a time in childhood when he was given a small compass and became fascinated with the magnetic dial. Maybe your child sits down at the piano and becomes absorbed in making different sounds. Or perhaps he begs for a watercolor set or a basketball. Maybe he makes huge messes in the basement with a chemistry set or has an engine out in the back yard that he loves to tinker with. Take these things seriously. Your child may be telling you about a special talent or ability that deserves cultivation.

Positive qualities. What inner characteristics does your child have? This is the most subtle of the four areas but ultimately the most important. Note any of the following traits you've observed in him: compassion, patience, persistence, loyalty, generosity, courage, faith, honor, ingenuity, creativity, friendliness, wisdom, intuition, will, playfulness, wonder, curiosity, adventurousness. While most of these attributes can't be measured by standardized tests, they may be the "secret ingredients" that carry him into life as a successful person—if, that is, they're recognized and nurtured by an understanding adult.

Nurturing the Positive

Once you've identified a long list of positive qualities in your child's life, go to work highlighting them at home and at school. This will help to reverse the vicious cycle of learning failure or learning boredom—where negatives are foreground and positives are hidden. Shift the focus away from the disabilities, deficiencies, and deficits in your child's learning life and concentrate on the abilities, assets, and advantages. There are many creative ways to do this. Make sure he has a special place at home—a bulletin board, a shelf space, or a section of a room—where special achievements such as awards, trophies, photos, school papers, and projects can be proudly displayed. Take time at dinner to listen to him share the positive events that occurred that day. Read *100 Ways to Enhance Self-Concept in the Classroom* by Jack Canfield and Harold Wells or *Your Child's Self-Esteem* by Dorothy Corkille Briggs for many other fine suggestions.

More important than any specific activities you do with your child, however, is the attitude you have toward his capabilities as a learner. If you truly believe that there's something wrong with his brain, that he's a handicapped learner, or that he'll never be the great student his Uncle Joe was, then you'll get the performance and behavior to match your beliefs. Kids are very good at complying with our expectations. On the other hand, if you really believe in him, there's no telling how far he can go.

Steering Clear of Excessive Praise

Avoid lavish positive reinforcement of a child's special talents. This could make your child feel just as uncomfortable as when everybody was pointing out his shortcomings, especially when done around his peers. Psychologist Stanley Krippner reports of a teacher who noticed a boy's exceptional artistic talent and proceeded to put up many of his drawings, only to have the other boys in the class dismiss his abilities as "sissy." He never drew after that. Kids also get suspicious when parents or teachers suddenly begin pouring on the praise and may pick up on the fact that they're using it as a new "technique" to enhance self-esteem. Make sure your praise is genuine and be sensitive in how you express it.

Using Interests and Abilities as Learning Tools

Make the strengths you've identified work for your child in learning things that are difficult for him. I once tutored a child who could not remember his math facts. He happened to be obsessed at the time with becoming a big league basketball player—he was only nine years old—and spent hours out on his backyard court making free throws. So, instead of hunching over flash cards and worksheets, we went outside and he dribbled the ball, counting as he bounced, and shot a basket every sixth step until he reached 60. In this way, he began to learn the 6's of the times tables.

If your child loves cars and hates to read, find books about cars. If he plays the piano and can't add, use the keys of the piano as a number line for doing mathematical computations. If he wants to be a movie star when he grows up and avoids writing, help him write a little movie script to practice.

One word of caution here. If there's even the slightest hint that your efforts in this direction are backfiring and he begins to avoid an activity that he previously loved, then stop what you're doing immediately! Children don't like to be coerced, and your child might resent your efforts to get him to do something he hates by mixing it with a favorite hobby or activity. But if you introduce an area of need into his personal world of interests and abilities in small doses and discover signs of excitement and progress in learning, you can rest assured that you're on the right track.

The Myth of Normality

Don't expect your child to learn according to some universal "norm." The main point of this book is that each child has his own personal way of learning which must be honored and nurtured. Parents often want and expect their kids to be normal. But the more we learn about individual differences, the more we realize that there is no such thing as a "normal" child. This concept of normality comes out of such statistical artifacts as the bell-shaped curve that psychologists use to plot test scores. Educators and psychologists construct tests to conform to this all-holy curve—where most people must score in the average range (the high point of the curve) and fewer people score at the extremes.

When IQ tests were first being developed, it turned out that girls consistently scored higher than boys on many of the items. In order to make things equal, testers threw out items that favored girls until a normal bell curve was attained for all children. Diane McGuinness, a University of South Florida psychologist, says that there are basic neuropsychological differences between the sexes—with boys generally superior on visual-spatial aptitude and girls better in verbal ability. She suggests that if the test makers took these gender differences into account when constructing their assessments—instead of making the data conform to some statistical ideal—"overnight millions of disabled boys would become normal readers."

It's also important to point out that in addition to gender differences, there are many other variables that make the concept of universal normality a myth. Who is to say that one child's blend of abilities/disabilities is any more or less normal than another child's? Ridding ourselves of these unreal concepts of normality allows us to see children as they really are—and not in terms of some artificial standard.

Letting Children Bloom in Their Own Way

Don't make your child "live up" to your expectations. Your high expectations for your child may have more to do with your own ambitions than his. Perhaps you were a poor math student. You may want him to attain success in mathematics and reach a goal you were never able to achieve. On the other hand, you may be an avid book lover and expect him to read at an early age. The German psychoanalyst Alice Miller points out in her book *The Drama of the Gifted Child* how destructive it can be when parents try to live out their own lives through their children. Miller calls this a subtle form of emotional child abuse.

You need to believe in your child *on his own terms*. In many cases, his hopes, dreams, ambitions, loves, and abilities won't coincide with yours. In fact, it may be difficult for you even to recognize his talents because of this very fact. That's why you need to gather information from a wide range of sources—teachers, relatives, your child's friends, professionals, and neighbors—digesting what you learn as objectively as possible.

Ultimately, it's your child himself who will tell you what he is capable of and how he learns best. Listen carefully to his deepest self-expressions and you will discover who he really is and where he wants to go in his life. Then it's up to both of you to work toward these goals—to help your child in his own way. In the next chapter, we'll explore the importance of helping children move along this inner pathway in their own time, as well, and we'll look at how destructive it can be when parents expect too much too soon from their late blooming children.

CHAPTER 11

A Patient Attitude: Honoring Your Child's Learning Rate

TEACHER: "Monitors are you ready yet? . . . All ready girls, you have no time to waste. Now I'm waiting. . . . All right hurry up, you take too long on these problems. It should only take you about five minutes."

*T*hirty years ago, American anthropologist Jules Henry observed that "American children work almost constantly under the lash of time." Henry's words are even more true today. Time rules not only the school day of American school children but their entire developmental history. Beginning at their child's birth, parents start the clock, nervously awaiting the time when she first sits up, crawls, walks, and says her first words. They read child development books that give the ages at which a normal child acquires skills, and they compare notes with their friends and relatives concerning the rate at which other children are achieving these same milestones. Any delay from the norm gets viewed with alarm. To hedge against this, parents flock to programs that promise to "teach your baby to read, write, and do math" in the belief that earlier means better.

When children enter kindergarten, the curriculum—a Latin word meaning "racetrack"—begins. "Readiness" programs prepare them for reading, writing, and math skills. Then, somewhere in the middle of first grade, parents (and now, too, teachers) check their watches again. If their children are not reading, a little buzzer goes off saying "Something's wrong!" and remedial programs enter the picture. Parents and teachers rarely consider the possibility that children may have their own internal clocks, ticking to the tock of a different timetable.

Concern is growing among child development researchers that we're forcing our children into academic work even earlier than kindergarten or first grade. A joint statement issued by the National Association for the Education of Young Children (NAEYC) and the National Association of Elementary School Principals urges preschools to reduce their heavy emphasis upon academically-oriented and teacher-centered education. David Elkind, president of NAEYC, points out that the push over the past two decades to maximize a child's potential at an early age has created a situation where preschool children are being given a watered-down version of the first-through-third-grade curriculum. This often results in premature learning problems due to inappropriate teaching methods. Yet children don't realize this and blame themselves for their failure to learn. In his best-selling book *The Hurried Child*, Elkind emphasizes the importance of letting children grow in their own time, with plenty of opportunities to engage in free play, fantasy, and sensory-motor experiences; activities that provide the basic building blocks for *later* academic work. This chapter will underline what Elkind and others have said about the "hurried child" syndrome in our country, and suggest practical ways that parents can help their children become achievers without rushing them into academics before their time.

Slowness as a Virtue

We live in a culture that worships speed. From fast cars to fast food, velocity is the American way of life. We esteem the individual who can make "snap judgments." We refer to intelligent people as "quick." In the schoolroom, we favor children who have their hands up first, are the first done on a test, and are the first to read, write, or compute.

The reality is that different children learn at vastly different rates. Some children learn to read at age three while others don't learn until age nine or later. Unfortunately, our society considers six or seven—and increasingly now even four or five—to be "the age" at which reading must occur. The child who learns to read "on time" is accepted as normal. However the "late bloomers" are in serious trouble. For although they develop in a perfectly acceptable way in accordance with their own particular patterns of development, they will be the ones to earn the labels *learning disabled, educationally handicapped, underachiever,* and *dyslexic.* To be slow means to be dumb, or literally, retarded.

Yet, in other cultures, slowness is a virtue. The person who acts quickly is regarded with disdain in many Eastern countries where businessmen sit for days contemplating a business decision before taking any action. It's a sign of bad manners to be on time for a meeting in some Middle Eastern countries. Even in Western Europe there's a slower pace of life than in the United States. Anthropologist Edward T. Hall wrote: "Many of my European subjects observed that in Europe human relationships are important whereas in the United States the schedule is important."

These cultural differences are reflected in the classroom. In a comparison of beginning reading methods in fourteen countries, the United States had the narrowest "critical period" during which a child had to learn to read or be considered a disabled learner. Such countries as Norway, Sweden, and Denmark provide much greater leeway in this critical period and as a consequence have fewer problem readers.

The Advantages of Being a
Late Bloomer

Most American classrooms expose six and seven year olds to the fine print of blackboards, basal readers, and worksheets; require them to listen to teacher instruction for several hours a day; and confine them to desks for long periods of time. Yet, many of these children simply aren't ready for this. Dr. Louise Bates Ames, associate director of the Gesell Institute in New Haven, Connecticut, suggested that if we let children enter first grade based on their own developmental readiness, rather than according to when they were born (the usual method of determining placement) we might eliminate up to 50 percent of all learning disabilities in this country.

In many cases, children entering first grade—not to mention those in kindergarten or preschool—don't have the auditory and visual discrimination skills necessary for the demands of classroom reading and listening. Reviewing research on vision from the 1930s on, Raymond and Dorothy Moore, in their book *Better Late Than Early,* suggest that "there is strong evidence that a child's eyes are not physiologically ready for continual and consistent reading until he is at least 8 or even older." Citing the work of Joseph Wepman, a noted researcher in the area of auditory skills in childhood, the Moores observed that some children cannot easily discriminate certain phonetic sounds until the end of their eighth year.

Many normal kindergarten and first grade youngsters don't have the thinking skills to adequately perform the tasks given to them by their teachers. Jean Piaget pointed out that children go through four fundamental stages of cognitive development as they mature: sensorimotor, preoperational, concrete operations, and formal operations. Children cannot understand certain academic skills—including arithmetic—until they have achieved at least the concrete operations stage. In many children this occurs around six years of age. Different children, however, arrive at this developmental milestone at different ages. During the 1960s, when American educators debated about how schools could accelerate children through these stages, Piaget humorously referred to this urge for speed as "the American question." He emphasized that it was not important to him how *fast* children went through these stages, but, more important, how thoroughly they became engaged at each step along the way.

Some educators even go so far as to say that *most* children would be better off if they postponed academic learning until later on in their school lives. Sixty-five years ago, Rudolf Steiner, the founder of Waldorf Education, criticized the tendency of parents and teachers to rush the teaching of reading and writing. Steiner observed: "Reading and writing as we have them today are really not suited to the human being 'til a later age, in the eleventh or twelfth year, and the more one is blessed with not being able to read and write well before this age, the better it is for the later years of life."

Parents will, of course, balk at the idea of their children not reading until the age of eight or nine, to say nothing of eleven or twelve years of age. Yet in some cases, they have no choice but to wait, since attempts at remediation before that time will often bear little fruit. A Wisconsin mother wrote me about her seven-year-old child. This boy couldn't read, wrote many words backwards, and had coordination problems. Rather than put him in a special program—he'd been in one as a four year old—they decided to home school him. By the age of nine, he'd developed a fascination with reading, became an ace in badminton, and according to his mother could "never get enough math problems to work."

Another mother took her son out of a special education program—where he was miserable—and put him in an alternative school that didn't put a great deal of importance on early reading skills. Her son went through the second and third grades without learning to read. She sometimes became worried about this. The school reassured her: "I remember being told, look, some kids don't learn how to read until they are in third or fourth grade. That's just the way it is. You can't push it. Then they hate reading whenever they do learn to read. Well, by the end of the fourth grade, miraculously, Ricky could read."

Some students won't even learn to read until they leave school. Here, for example, is an account of one student who attended the well-known alternative school Summerhill, as told by its founder, A. S. Neill: "There was Jack, a boy who could not learn to read. No one could teach Jack. Even when he asked for a reading lesson, there was some hidden obstruction that kept him from distinguishing between *b* and *p*, *l* and *k*. He left school at seventeen without the ability to read. . . . Today, Jack is an expert toolmaker. He loves to talk about metalwork. He can read now. . . . He mainly reads articles about mechanical things—and sometimes he reads works on psychology."

The Art of Patience: Some Guidelines

Given that some children won't naturally learn to read, write, spell, or do math until after first grade, the big question for parents becomes: "What do I do in the meantime?" This is a crucial question, since most school systems don't stop to watch kids smell the roses along the way, but cling to timetables for achievement and deposit those kids who aren't keeping step into programs for handicapped learners or remedial groups in regular classrooms. Many parents have relatives and friends breathing down their necks as well, wondering why David can't do the things that *their* Sally can do.

First of all, it isn't enough to simply say "Leave him alone, he'll grow out of it" and let it go at that. This is the easy way out for parents and teachers faced with a difficult dilemma. The truth is that he *will* grow out of it, but *only* if he's given the proper support and nurturance at home and at school.

The Importance of Faith

Trust that your child really *will* learn in his own time. Because late bloomers do not bloom at the age or time they are supposed to, doubt may creep into the minds of the gardeners/parents that their children will never bloom. Parents need to have an almost sacred faith in the processes of life and growth, especially when they feel anxiety, frustration, or intense impatience because their late blooming children are not developing according to their standard of progress.

You wouldn't sit in front of a plant and get angry at it for not growing faster. So why do the same thing to a human being? To parents who truly despair, I offer this wonderful little passage from the Sufi musician Hazrat Inayat Khan: "And when a person says, 'Oh I have waited and waited and waited but my ship never comes' he is keeping his ship back, . . . But the one who does not even see the ship but says 'It is coming, it is coming' is calling it and it will come." Remember from the last chapter how important our hidden expectations can be to a child's growth.

Give yourself a period of time during which you will make a commitment not to be overly concerned about your child's academic progress. You can determine this time span according to your own desires, but I suggest you make it as broad as possible, extending to at least age eight and better yet to age nine or ten. Then, if your child still hasn't learned to read, write, spell, or do math in spite of your best efforts to gently support and nurture the process, you can begin to worry. All too often, parents push the panic button much too early, when their children reach age six or seven—and sometimes even earlier. Louise Bates Ames writes of one child whose parents brought him to the Gesell Institute because they were worried he might be learning disabled. Their belief was based on the fact that the little chap wasn't so good at writing his letters and numbers. He had just turned four years of age!

Recognizing a Blossom When You See One

Think of late blooming in broader terms than just reading, writing, and arithmetic. People like A. S. Neill's Jack, who don't learn to read until adulthood, do bloom—but not necessarily academically. Some parents may need to stop equating blooming with success in the three Rs. For a few children, especially bodily-kinesthetic or spatial learners, blooming in life may have more to do with achieving success in artistic, mechanical, or athletic areas.

Blooming may also involve learning to acquire the three Rs in alternative ways. The child who has problems with arithmetic may learn to use a calculator. The nonreader may learn to use a tape recorder, typewriter, or computer. Norman and Margaret Silberberg have suggested that schools set up a "bookless curriculum" for these kids. By establishing a different criterion to define blooming, we can make it easier for certain children to grow and develop along the pathways that are most in tune with their inner capabilities.

Provide models of late blooming for your child. If your child is young, read her *Leo the Latebloomer*, a charming story about a little lion who came into his own after a long period of waiting. Older children might enjoy hearing about famous people who bloomed late, including Albert Einstein, Thomas Edison, and Winston Churchill. Adolescents could perhaps relate better to contemporary celebrities such as Cher, Bruce Jenner, and Tom Cruise—individuals who achieved success in a certain field yet had great difficulty with academic skills.

Respecting the Garden of Childhood

Provide your child with plenty of opportunities to enjoy childhood. Reading, writing, math, and other abstract activities hurry kids out of the garden of childhood with its carefree games, wonderful imaginative life, and spontaneous play. Several recent books, including David Elkind's *The Hurried Child*, Marie Winn's *Children without Childhood*, and Neil Postman's *The Disappearance of Childhood*, suggest that we're rushing children prematurely into the tasks and responsibilities of adulthood. Anthropologist Ashley Montagu observed in his book *Growing Young* that it may be to our advantage biologically to retain as much of our youth as possible into adulthood. As long as late-blooming children aren't going to be reading early anyway, you might as well let them enjoy these golden days while they last. Don't schedule lots of readiness activities for them. Let them choose their activities themselves, but provide them with the right environmental supports: playgrounds, nature experiences, art supplies, puppets and costumes, and toys and games of all kinds. They will often instinctively be drawn to the materials that help them prepare for the skills of literacy.

Realize that a child's natural course of development does not follow a predictably even path. Children typically grow in fits and spurts, through periods of stagnation and periods of discovery, times of flare-up and times of quietude. Our schools generally do not provide environments that are sensitive to the ups and downs of growth. Schools tend to identify children as problem learners when they are in their "down" times—intervening in such a way that they are identified for many years to come on the basis of what might more likely have been a fleeting phase in the entire pattern of their development. If your child happens to be in a valley right now, it's entirely possible that a mountain is just around the corner.

Even if your child is an "on-time bloomer" or an "early bloomer," you still should be concerned about the current educational trend to push children prematurely into academic learning. Such early pressures on children to achieve may cause stresses that can result in emotional or physical problems later on down the line. In *The Hurried Child*, David Elkind describes the fate of gifted children pushed beyond their limits at too early an age, only to burn out before they even reach adulthood. Earl Ogletree, a Chicago State University professor, suggests that premature exposure to abstract thinking, even in so-called normal children, runs the risk of disturbing the child's subtle energy systems—called *ki* in Chinese acupuncture or *bioplasma* in Russian parapsychology—which can result in physical deterioration later on in life.

This doesn't mean that if your child eagerly takes to reading as a four year old you should be alarmed and hide the books. I once asked John Holt what he thought about Rudolf Steiner's belief that children shouldn't read until they're at least seven, and he emphatically replied: "Children should read when they want to." The important word here is when *they* want to not when *you* want them to. If reading, writing, and math skills come out of a child's own exhuberance about learning, then it's clearly time for him to bloom academically. However, what we see happening across the country with current attempts at early education looks too often like parents and teachers attempting to foist academic learning on children because of their own concerns about keeping up with the Joneses or enhancing their prestige as super-parents. Children become victims of our own self-importance when we push them in this way.

Finally, I want to repeat that you not simply throw up your hands and say "O.K., I'll leave my child alone until he's seven years old." In the chapter on relationships, I pointed out how you are *always* educating your child, whether you know it or not. It's extremely important for parents to provide *appropriate* learning experiences for their children based on their interests and needs. During the first seven years of life, that especially means lots of opportunities to engage in sensory exploration. In the next chapter, we'll examine how the education of the senses should provide the basis, not only for learning during the first seven years of life, but also for much of a child's formal academic learning during the years that follow.

CHAPTER 12

The Doors of Perception: Helping Children Come Back to Their Senses

*T*he senses pervade our lives just as they permeate our language: "Can you *hear* what I'm trying to say?" "I *see* what you mean." "Let me *touch* on that issue for a moment." "I can almost *taste* victory." "He's trying to *sniff* out the competition." In fact, the senses serve as the bedrock of our entire existence. As adults, our feelings and ideas often seem far away from the sensory world, yet if we traced the origins of thought back far enough, as Piaget and others have done, we would always come back to the senses as the raw material of far more complex forms of consciousness.

For the infant the senses are everything. Unlike the interior world of the adult whose hours are filled with subjective ramblings, each moment of an infant's life is lived on the outside, as it were, in direct contact with the textures, timbres, and tessellations of the sensual world. Learning takes place in the midst of this perceptual universe. Only by seeing, touching, tasting, smelling, and hearing the objects of the external world can the infant construct a model of reality that will serve as a basis for more abstract learning later on in life.

The Unified Senses Theory

Most children before the age of five or six do not experience five clearly distinct senses. Instead, the senses tend to flow into each other. This phenomenon—known as *synaesthesia*—is far more common in childhood than is currently believed. Heinz Werner, one of the country's greatest developmental psychologists, suggested that "instances of synaesthesia can be found in almost any carefully written diary of observations on child behavior. He offers examples including a six year old's description of "light and dark-red whistling" and the "gold and silver striking of the hour." This mixing of the senses drops off considerably as children grow older with one study measuring about 13 percent of an adult population to be gifted with chromatism—or color hearing—whereas 50 percent of children measured had this capacity.

The senses also appear to be highly fused to feeling and dynamic action in the young child. Werner called this form of holistic sensory experience *physiognomic perception*. He wrote: "All of us, at some time or other, have had this experience. A landscape, for instance, may be seen suddenly in immediacy as expressing a certain mood—it may be gay or melancholy or pensive. This mode of perception differs radically from the more everyday perception in which things are known according to their 'geometrical-technical,' matter-of-fact qualities." He illustrated this form of perception by citing the case of a boy who at two-and-a-half years of age called a towel hook a "cruel thing" and at three-and-a-half years old thought that the number 5 looked "mean" while the number 4 appeared to be "soft." A four-year-old girl, upon seeing some cards on which certain angular pictures were drawn, exclaimed, "Ugh! What a lot of prickles and thorns!" and refused to pick up the cards fearing she would be injured by them. The world to young children is alive with vital energy, purpose, and drive.

As children grow up, they usually abandon this rich sensory experience. Adults begin to give children labels for things, and the verbal name of an object overshadows its vivid perceptual immediacy. Parents caution, "Don't touch," "Don't stare," "Don't be an eavesdropper," and in other ways discourage children's highly active sensory exploration. Teachers focus greatest attention in school on pure auditory and visual information, while providing few opportunities for smelling, tasting, touching, or experimenting in ways that combine all of the senses.

Most children silently submit to this socialization process. Five distinct senses emerge after a few years that operate in isolation from emotion and physical action. Children learn to emphasize hearing and seeing over feeling, touching, smelling, and tasting. They meet with a world of abstract symbols and learn how to accommodate their blunted perceptual organs to these new requirements.

Some children don't make this transition quite as easily. Children with unique learning styles often perceive the world in multisensory, synaesthetic, or physiognomic ways. Their sensory apparatus hasn't fragmented into separate perceptual channels. You may recall Billy from Chapter 1, who described his thought processes as a combination of music and architecture, or the boy at the beginning of Chapter 6, who needed to move and listen at the same time. In actuality, each and every child has his own unique perceptual style. Regardless of the specific pattern, most youngsters' senses are organized in ways different from the expectations of society, and often parents or teachers don't have a clear idea of how to reach and teach them in their own way.

Sacrificial Lambs: Giving Away One's Ears and Eyes

As a result of their unique sensory capacities, some children get diagnosed as "perceptually handicapped." Neurologists, psychologists, and special educators create "learning sicknesses" for them with names such as "auditory association dysfunction," "visual memory deficit," and so on. These kids are supposed to be seeing twisted symbols, backwards letters, and all sorts of other perceptual oddities. The reality is that most of these children perceive the world just fine—*from their own point of view.* What trips them up is the collision of their personal way of looking at the world with the expectations that others have about how they are to see the world.

What people call a learning disability should really be known as a *perceptual mismatch.* This idea became clear to me when I was reading about an experiment in R. L. Gregory's classic book on perception, *Eye and Brain.* In this experiment, a subject was instructed to complete a tracing task—staying within the boundaries of a double-lined star—and to write several words. In the first trial, he simply did the tasks normally. In the second trial, he did the tasks with his writing hand obscured so that he could only see what he was doing by looking at a television monitor. In the final trial, the television was tape delayed so that there was a half-second interval between writing and seeing what was written on the monitor.

In the first two trials, performance was more or less satisfactory. In the final trial, however, the performance was virtually illegible—looking very much like the work of a person labeled as a severe dyslexic. This experiment beautifully illustrates the internal state of many individuals labeled learning disabled. Like the subject in the experiment, so-called learning disabled people experience a conflict between two situations—their own immediate experience and one imposed from without. Caught between the two, a severe perceptual dissonance results and performance disintegrates.

Many children with special learning styles encounter a similar situation. They enter school only to find that their unique perceptions about things are not acknowledged or accepted, and they soon learn to mistrust them. In their efforts to adjust to the demands of a traditional curriculum, they give away their eyes and ears to parents and teachers who they feel know more than they do. Yet their sacrifice

ultimately works against them when they confront a persist-
ent gap between what they actually see and hear and what
others tell them they must perceive. This conflict creates
anxiety—or perhaps it would be better to say that this conflict *is* anxiety—and it results in the chaos that specialists
regard as the warning signs of hidden learning disability.

School stress may be responsible for many perceptual
problems affecting learning in millions of children nationwide. We now know that stress has a major impact on the
senses—dulling and distorting them in many ways. Ray
Gottlieb, a California optometrist and psychologist, suggests
that "a major cause of nearsightedness and other visual
problems is the tension generated by current methods of
education." He cites a Connecticut study where myopia was
reduced by 50 percent when multisensory education and
anxiety reduction techniques were used in classrooms.
Helmer Myklebust, a well-known authority on the role of
hearing in learning, points to what he calls "psychic deaf-
ness" in certain children, stemming from emotional trauma.
In each case, demands placed upon children that are beyond
their control serve to distort perceptual abilities that are
crucial to academic success.

It's rather easy to create learning disabilities in a whole
population of schoolchildren by establishing a conflict between perception and expectation. This was actually done
when an instructor asked a group of elementary schoolchildren to make paper airplanes as a part of an experiment.
Everyone got to work and after ten minutes of intense activity made many different kinds of planes—all working just
fine.

Then the instructor asked them to put their planes away
and to follow *his* directions. He led them through a step-by-
step method for creating a paper airplane. After a few minutes, most of the class was totally confused and the floor was
littered with botched attempts at plane making. In this experiment, children were presented with an official version of
doing something that conflicted with their own personal

knowledge. The result was frustration and failure, or—in pedagoguese—"sensorimotor dysfunction." Tim Gallwey, author of several books on peak performance in sports, puts it more succinctly: "The more 'how-to-do-it' a learner receives, the likelier he is to get in his own way."

Beyond Short Circuits and Crossed Wires: Some Guidelines

Children must be allowed to experience their *own* perceptions—and not someone else's expectations for how they are to perceive—in order to fully realize their true potential. Parents and teachers should put aside much of the foolishness they've heard about learning disabilities and their relationship to "short circuits," "crossed wires," and malfunctioning sensory channels. It equates kids with robots and reminds me of the science cartoons I used to watch as a child that showed a little man inside the brain at a switchboard controlling all the nerve impulses and brain functions.

The human brain is far more flexible, adaptable, and complex than these elementary models lead us to believe. Even more important than human neurology is the human spirit—that part of our being Arthur Koestler called "the ghost in the machine"—which has suffered neglect in all the hue and cry about remediation of learning problems. Each child is a human being with a unique set of perceptions about the world. If we're ever going to help kids find their own competencies, we must start taking their own way of looking at things more seriously. Instead of trying to change them with all the latest remediation techniques, we need to find out more about the sensory world in which they live, and then help them to learn according to their own perceptual styles.

Education Through All the Senses

Provide your child with plenty of opportunities for multi-sensory learning. Children are in their element when surrounded by things they can simultaneously hear, see, touch, taste, and smell. Maureen Murdock, a California therapist and educator, writes: "Some people find, to their great surprise, that they can 'see' an entire page that they were studying if they smell the scent of the flowers present in the room while they were studying. Or a complex math formula may be recalled by its thorny texture!"

Provide your child with brightly colored paper for writing assignments. Supply her with scratch-and-sniff books or books with unusually textured paper. Mix up pudding or other creamy foods to use as finger paint in writing words and numbers, or help her create letters out of bread dough. Use Cheerios, raisins, or peanuts as counters in doing math. Vicki Cobb's book *Science Experiments You Can Eat* suggests many delicious ways of learning about the properties of the physical world. Act as a "guide" for your blindfolded child during walks in nature where she can attend to the sounds, smells, and textures of the outdoors. Provide a sensory-rich play environment; with optical illusions; smell bottles (little film containers with different scents inside); texture boards (plywood with rug swatches, silk, rubber, felt, and other tactile materials attached to its surface); and sound boxes (sealed boxes with mystery sounds inside). Allow kids to engage in natural multisensory experiences including cooking, building dams and forts, water play, creative movement, dramatic improvisation, and such tactile art activities as clay sculpting or making three-dimensional collages.

"Mistakes" May Be Misunderstandings

When your child perceives something in a different way than you do, before correcting her, ask her to tell you a

little about it. We're so quick to correct children's errors that often their real meaning—reflecting an inner perception of children's personal reality—evades us. It's important to keep in mind that Jean Piaget began his illustrious career as a child researcher in the Paris laboratories of Alfred Binet when he became fascinated with the meaning behind the *errors* children made on early intelligence tests.

An Alabama mother writes about her son's own curious brand of sensory logic: "When Adam was almost three he told his father, 'My cold leg hurts.' His dad asked, 'Is your leg cold?' Adam said, 'No! My cold leg has a scratch on it.' If you don't understand the logic of what he was trying to say, go to the bathroom sink and turn on the cold water. Our bathroom is right by the hot water heater, and it is very important to know which hand turns on which faucet. At times when he can't understand right and left, we use 'hot side' and 'cold side.' He gets it every time." The mother tells of her own confusion as a child in school when asked to raise her right hand. She held up her *write* hand (she was left-handed) and couldn't understand why people laughed at her.

Similarly, when children reverse letters and numbers there may be an underlying perceptual reason why they do this. John Holt suggested that for many youngsters who reverse, it simply doesn't make any difference which way the letter is pointing. Holt commented: "To be told that a 'backwards' *P* that they have drawn is 'wrong' or that it isn't a *P* at all, must be very confusing and even frightening. If you can draw a horse, or dog, or cat, or car pointing any way you want, why can't you draw a *P* or *B* or *E* any way you want?" Children who reverse letters need to be carefully initiated into the realization that letters are different from pictures. But this can only happen *after* you acknowledge that your child's own perceptions are legitimate.

Sensory Obstacles to Learning

Make sure your child is free from specific perceptual impairments that can block his learning. Children who can't see the front of the classroom or hear the teacher's instructions won't learn what is being taught. Symptoms to watch out for include eye rubbing, squinting, looking with one eye, straining to hear, watching the teacher's lips, asking for directions over and over again, and headaches or eye strain after short periods of reading. If you suspect that your child may have minor hearing or seeing problems affecting his school performance, consult with your family physician or a qualified optometrist or audiologist to have him evaluated. Sometimes eyeglasses or a hearing aid will correct the problem.

Often the problem may be more subtle, involving choppy eye movements that make it hard for a child to follow words across a page, or hearing loss at specific frequencies that affects his ability to tell the difference between certain sounds in language—for example, "bit" and "bet." Behavioral optometrists can help eliminate some visual problems through the use of specially designed optical training exercises that coordinate and relax eye muscles. Audiologists or speech and language therapists can engage children in activities designed to increase their sensitivity to subtle auditory changes in the language.

Here are some simple exercises that your child can do at home to unblock and de-stress the senses for academic learning. To help his eyes focus and move quickly across a printed page, have him select an old book or magazine and, beginning at the top of the page, circle or color in all the "o"s (or three-letter words, letters with stems pointing downward, capital letters, or words beginning with "m") *in order* for a specific period of time—let's say, three minutes. When doing this activity—or when reading for meaning at any time—allow him to use his finger or a pencil to follow words across the page. Some parents and teachers still think that "word pointing" is a bad thing, but speed-reading teachers will tell you that the use of the finger to guide the eye—with the finger always moving faster than the eye—is a key to rapid reading.

If your child experiences fatigue after reading, have him do the following exercise to relax his eyes:

Palming

- Take off glasses, hats, or other obstructions around the eyes.
- Sit upright in a straight-backed chair with relaxed posture and a straight spine and neck.
- Rub your hands together until they are warm.
- Cup the palms of your hands and place one over each eye, palms inward, so that the heels of your palms touch your cheekbones. *Do not press or rub up against the eyes at any time!*
- Close your eyes and begin gently massaging the muscles around your eyes. Use a table as a support for your elbows if your arms get tired. Feel the spaces behind and around your eyes getting loose and relaxed. Let your jaw and shoulders drop a bit as you relax them, too.
- When you feel ready to stop, open your eyes slowly and continue to feel the relaxation in and around your eyes as you return to your reading.

Millions of children in China do exercises similar to this one every day before beginning their academic work at school.

To heighten auditory awareness, read passages that have unusual sound patterns or changes in inflection including nonsense poetry by Lewis Carroll, Ogden Nash, and Shel Silverstein. Bill Martin's *Sounds of Language* is an excellent reading series that focuses on playfulness with the auditory patterns of language. Work out auditory codes for communicating messages around the house. For example, three long whistles might mean come to dinner, or a short whistle and a long whistle could indicate time for bed. Turn off the television and suggest that your child listen to the radio, or tell stories and sing songs together as a family. Each of these activities will help your child become more sensitive to the auditory dimensions of language.

Whatever means you choose to use in enriching your child's sensory world, it's important to keep in mind that you aren't trying to *change* the way in which he perceives, but to help him use the sensory abilities he already possesses in a way that helps, rather than hinders, him. Too many children suffer from learning frustration, not because of their own sensory dysfunction, but because inappropriate educational methods and cultural influences rip them away from their perceptual roots. When we bring these kids back to their senses, their learning capacities really begin to unfold. Of course, adverse environmental influences sometimes cloud the senses and impair learning. Such factors as improper food, harsh light, polluted air, and excessive noise may distort sensory information coming into a child from the outside world. We'll look at the important question of learning ecology in the next chapter.

CHAPTER 13

The Ecology of Learning: Providing Your Child With a Nurturing Environment

*M*rs. Carlson got the news on Thursday. Her son Paul had just gotten his report card—liberally sprinkled with "Cs," "Ds," and even a couple of "Fs." On Friday she received a call from his teacher. Paul was being considered for testing because of his poor performance. During the weekend Mrs. Carlson thought things over. Why was Paul doing so badly at school? Had she failed him as a parent? Was it his teacher's fault? Did he have a learning disability?

The answer may be none of the above. In fact, during the next week, as Mrs. Carlson looked more carefully at Paul's learning environment, she began to get a better picture of why her son might be doing so badly in his schoolwork. On Monday she noticed a stash of candy bars in Paul's room and she recalled something she'd read concerning how chocolate and sugar can get in the way of effective learning. On Tuesday she kept track of how Paul was spending his after-school hours and realized that television was winning out over homework five hours to one. On Wednesday she visited his classroom and discovered one helpless teacher and thirty-five noisy kids trying to learn in a room with flickering neon lights, chalk dust, drab green carpets, and the noise of jets taking off and landing overhead every five minutes—the school was next to the municipal airport. On Thursday Mrs. Carlson took stock of her investigations, and it became very clear to her that the *environment,* as much as anything else, was in need of restructuring if Paul was to be helped in his efforts to become a better learner.

There's been a lot of research undertaken over the last twenty years in the area of the learning ecology, yet the field itself is still relatively unknown in educational circles. While the media frequently report on the influence of nutrition in learning, few parents, teachers, and school administrators seem to be aware of the impact of other ecological factors such as light, color, air, sound, space, and time on attention, motivation, and behavior in educational settings at home and at school.

The material on learning ecology presented here applies to all children, but it may be particularly relevant to those youngsters who are experiencing problems in learning at home or in school. Research suggests that many of these children may be chemically sensitive to environmental influences that make traditional classroom learning a chore.

What's Eating Johnny Is What Johnny's Eating: The Role of Diet in Learning

My visits to candy stores and fast-food outlets as a youngster were more like pilgrimages to sacred temples than trips to commercial establishments. For many children today this continues to be true. However, certain children can no longer afford to make the journey. The refined carbohydrates, colas, and synthetic substances that go into their bodies when they visit these places affect their ability to concentrate, remember, and behave. With breakfasts of sugar-laden cereals and syrupy pancakes, lunches of white bread and chemically treated meats, and dinners of minimal protein and maximum dessert, home and school environments often do little to improve the situation.

Some children seem to do just fine with whatever goes into their mouths at the table. Other youngsters, however, appear to be biochemically vulnerable—for whatever reason in nature or nurture—and develop any number of symptoms including red, swollen, or baggy eyes; headaches or stomachaches; restless behavior a couple of hours after eating; specific cravings for foods; chronic fatigue; and constant coughing, sneezing, or sniffling. These symptoms can affect school performance by clogging up children's eyes and ears, fogging their brains, and kicking up their bodies' energetic systems to a frenzied pitch or dragging them down to the depths of lethargy. Naturally, you should consult a medical doctor when any of these symptoms persist. However, if no clear-cut medical problem can be detected after a thorough exam, then consider the following possibilities.

Food Allergies

Certain children are allergic to foods they eat every day. In fact, some doctors suggest that allergenic foods are often a person's favorite foods. The most common culprits include wheat, milk, corn, beef, chocolate and cola, eggs, coffee and tea, certain citrus fruits, and foods containing chemical additives. In order to determine whether your child is allergic to a given food or set of foods, it's best to work with a medical specialist called a *clinical ecologist*. These doctors help parents set up "elimination diets." Diets of this type remove all potentially offending foods for several days while the doctor observes the child's behavior for signs of improvement. After a time, the doctor systematically reintroduces selected foods into the diet one at a time, with parent and doctor monitoring the child for any sign of a recurrence of the symptoms. Finally, after the doctor identifies the specific food allergies, she sets up a "rotation diet" which allows the child to eat selected foods that he can tolerate. To prevent new allergic reactions from forming, the child is allowed these foods only every few days. Several self-help books assist parents in setting up specific programs for their children, including *Tracking Down Hidden Food Allergy* by William Crook and *Why Your Child is Hyperactive* by Ben Feingold.

Vitamin and Mineral Deficiencies

Recent studies suggest that many children labeled learning disabled or hyperactive have specific nutritional deficits. These include deficiencies of trace minerals such as zinc and calcium and lower levels of essential B vitamins. While a well-balanced diet can help redress these problems, some doctors advocate supplementing the diets of these youngsters with megadoses of specific vitamins and minerals, an approach referred to as orthomolecular medicine. This treatment should be carefully supervised by a medical doctor, since high doses of nutritional supplements can have toxic effects if improperly administered. See *Dr. Cott's Help for Your Learning Disabled Child: The Orthomolecular Treatment* by Alan Cott and *Nourishing Your Child* by Ray Wunderlich and Dwight Kalita for more information.

Unstable Blood Sugar Levels

A diet heavy in refined sugar and other processed carbohydrates plays havoc with certain children's metabolic systems. The quick chemical transformation of these substances in the digestive tract sends blood sugar levels sky high and gets the adrenaline pumping—creating a mood elevation that can border on mania. The body's attempt to regain its chemical equilibrium leaves the adrenal glands exhausted and the blood sugar plummeting as the pancreas pumps out enough insulin to meet the high demand.

The result is a dopey, droopy, and dazed child. A child's specific blood sugar pattern can be measured through a Glucose Tolerance Test that involves a period of fasting, the drinking of several glasses of sugared water, and the measurement of blood sugar levels over several hours' time. Dr. Hugh Powers, a Texas pediatrician, contends that a child needn't be hypoglycemic (low blood sugar) to suffer from this condition. Remedies include identification of hidden food allergies, as well as the removal of sugars and refined carbohydrates from the diet—including white bread, noodles, rice, and potatoes—and their replacement with meals high in protein and complex carbohydrates: fish, poultry, lean meats, whole grains, legumes, seeds, and nuts. Many authorities also recommend intermittent snacking throughout the day to keep energy levels stable.

Your child may not suffer from food allergies, specific vitamin deficiencies, or unstable blood sugar levels. But, you would still do well to ensure a high quality diet, especially if there are learning problems in the background. That means eliminating candy and colas, substituting whole grains such as brown rice and whole wheat bread for starchy noodles and white bread, having lots of fresh fruit and vegetables available at lunch and dinner, and providing several high protein sources every day. Satisfy your child's sweet tooth by giving him desserts prepared with nuts, fruits, and other whole foods. See the book *S.N.A.C.K.S.: Speedy, Nutritious, and Cheap Kids' Snacks* by Jan Brink and Melinda Ramm for an excellent source of recipes.

Room to Move:
Space as an Ecological Variable

Perhaps you're familiar with scientific experiments on crowding where animals were packed together in a small space for a long period of time. These environments appeared to increase aggression, distress, and disease among the animals. We can draw some parallels with human populations—in this case, children in school. As Carole S. Weinstein, assistant professor of education at Rutgers, aptly put it some years ago: "Nowhere else [but in schools] are large groups of individuals packed so closely together for so many hours, yet expected to perform at peak efficiency on difficult learning tasks and to interact harmoniously." Weinstein's research revealed a number of factors associated with density in the learning place including nervousness, less social interaction, increased aggressiveness, and dissatisfaction. Maybe the children who aren't performing efficiently or interacting harmoniously are trying to tell us something about the environment in which they are failing.

The traditional elementary school is a masterpiece of architectural boredom: rectangular blackboards and bulletin boards surround straight rows of desks. The environment speaks for the consciousness it is attempting to cultivate in its students. Most youngsters willingly comply with this unnatural order of things, but a few either cannot or will not follow along. These are often the kinesthetic learners in class who need to move their bodies, touch things, and dynamically interact with the space they inhabit. In a static and linear classroom, kinesthetic kids all too often end up being spatially frustrated and exhibit hyperactive or aggressive behaviors. At home, too, many of these kids find themselves in environments where they have no space they can really call their own. There's simply no place for running, climbing, jumping, playing, or in other ways using space in creative ways.

The most successful classrooms and home learning environments have a number of spatial alternatives to allow for a broad spectrum of activity levels and styles, including open spaces for creative movement, physical games, and vigorous exercise; solo spaces where kids can go for privacy; and social spaces for interpersonal interaction, game playing, and group projects. See *Sunset Magazine*'s book *Things You Can Make for Children* for ideas on redoing your child's room or study area to allow for some of these possibilities.

Making Time for Learning:
The Temporal Factor

Children experience time in a different way than adults. Jean Piaget and his colleagues observed that for the child aged eight and younger, time passes much more slowly than for older people. A day is an eternity in the lives of young children, filled to the brim with activity and not segmented into minutes or hours. For some, this way of experiencing time persists past eight years of age. These youngsters have a lot of trouble fitting into a school environment where time is divided up into forty-minute periods, punctuated by a ringing bell. Many of them just start warming up to an activity when the period ends and it's time to move on to something new. They often have trouble remembering homework assignments, not because they're trying to be nasty or have poor memories, but because they operate according to C.S.T. (Children's Standard Time), which is essentially life in the present tense.

Children also have different temporal rhythms. The new field of chronopsychology provides us with information about the way in which human beings respond to internal patterns of time, including the daily circadian rhythms that regulate our sleep and waking cycles. We now know there is a biological basis for the common belief that certain people seem to be more active and alert in the morning ("larks"), while others take several hours to warm up and often don't reach their peak until late afternoon or evening ("owls"). The larks of the world have an easy time of it in school because they're all fresh and perky when the teacher is doing most of the instruction. The owls, on the other hand, reach their peak of alertness and concentration after school is out for the day. They may be the ones to end up identified as "tuned-out," underachieving, hyperactive, or learning disabled. We also know that there are ninety-minute cycles of attention in each individual, which alternate between poles of rest and activity, and possibly also between verbal and spatial orientation.

Pay attention to the time cycles of your child. See if you can identify peaks and valleys in attention during the day. Then build homework periods or other times of focused work around the peaks. If your child is an owl, afternoons or evenings may be the best time for learning. Tony Buzan, a superlearning educator, suggests that a study period last no longer than twenty to forty minutes. After forty minutes a person's learning curve begins to decline significantly. If study periods need to last longer than this, they ought to be punctuated by short breaks, perhaps using one of the relaxation exercises suggested in Chapter 8. Of course, if children are fully absorbed in an activity, they ought to be allowed to complete it, no matter how long it takes. Maria Montessori described this intense absorption of children as "the great work" and implored educators and parents to leave them alone when they are creatively engaged in this way.

Sound Mind, Sound Body: The Impact of Environmental Noise on Learning

Imagine a girl bent over her homework in the bedroom. Outside you hear her parents quarreling. Inside, a television in the corner blares out the latest sitcom while a stereo in the next room thumps in time to a rock beat. Down the street, the jackhammers noisily work on the city streets while trucks, buses, and cars go whizzing by. You wouldn't call this child learning disabled, underachieving, or tuned out because she couldn't produce acceptable work in this environment. You'd call her heroic for just trying!

Many children are similarly handicapped at home and school by the noises that surround them twenty-four hours a day. Dr. Sheldon Cohen and his associates at the University of Oregon studied elementary schools near Los Angeles

International Airport. They discovered that students in these schools had higher blood pressure and more difficulty solving mathematical problems and logical puzzles than control groups in non-airport areas. These children were also more likely to give up in frustration on school tasks earlier than the control groups.

Become aware of the different levels of background noise at home and at your child's school. Work to filter out harmful or distracting stimuli. At the same time seek to build in harmonious environmental sounds. This is especially true if your home or school is near an airport, a busy traffic intersection, or a noisy factory. Yet, even in a tranquil setting, there are internal noises to contend with—the constant low humming or buzzing of appliances, the activities of family members, the sounds of stereos, TVs, and radios. Where noises can't be eliminated, your child might wear soft foam earplugs available in most drugstores, or hearing protectors similar to those used by airport and construction workers. Bring soothing background sounds into the learning environment including relaxing music, recorded environmental sounds, and white sound generators. These efforts will provide your child with the "sound barrier" he needs to focus on learning tasks without interruption.

Full-Spectrum Education: Light and Color in the Learning Place

Virtually all elementary schools and many homes use cool-white fluorescent bulbs to provide the lighting under which millions of children study. Research suggests that this inexpensive source of artificial illumination may interfere with academic performance. One study equipped two elementary school classrooms with standard lighting fixtures, while two other rooms changed to full-spectrum fluorescent lighting, which includes a color spectrum closer to natural outdoor light. Experimenters made

time-lapse films of classroom sessions in thirty-minute seg-
ments once a month for six months and rated students
behaviorally. The children took academic tests three times
during this period. Full-spectrum lighting appeared to decrease the hyperactive behavior of students in the experi-
mental classrooms and also seemed to favorably influence
academic achievement.

Although full-spectrum lighting is several times more expensive than cool-white fluorescence, parents should be able
to afford at least one bulb for a child's study lamp and can
also make use of other light sources. Whenever possible,
place the study area near windows, and if full-spectrum
lighting is not available, use incandescent lamps as opposed
to traditional fluorescent fixtures. When using full-spectrum
lighting, make sure that it is properly equipped for radiation
protection so that potentially harmful ultraviolet waves will
get filtered out.

Color can also have a powerful influence on learning and
behavior. One study reported that children tested in rooms
they perceived as beautiful in color (light blue, yellow, yel-
low-green, or orange) scored twelve points higher on IQ
tests, while those tested in rooms rated ugly (white, black,
or brown) scored fourteen points lower than the norm. Ask
your child what his favorite colors are and then, with his
permission, put those hues around the study area at home.
Paint the walls or use posters, wall hangings, or other deco-
rations that include these harmonizing colors. At school,
teachers might take construction paper and line children's
study carrels or cover their desks. In her book *Unicorns Are
Real*, Florida educator Barbara Meister Vitale recommends
that children be able to select different colors as their own
moods change. She provides them with a wide assortment
of colors and allows them to select the ones that make them
feel calmer and more focused.

Clearing the Air for a Better Learning Atmosphere

We've learned a lot over the past few years about the negative short- and long-term effects of air pollution on physical health. Less well known is the impact of air pollution on learning. Lead, for example, may be implicated in the failure of some children to learn. Children absorb lead more easily than adults, one reason that lead exposure from crumbling paint chips in old buildings poses such a vicious threat to many children in this country. Smaller quantities of lead enter children's bodies through factory and car emissions and drinking water from leaded pipes. Because children ingest this lead in such minute quantities its effects are not immediately obvious. Yet a recent study suggested that lead and other metallic contaminants may be responsible in part for lower cognitive functioning in some children.

Other contaminants, such as tobacco smoke, ozone from smog, asbestos, formaldehyde from walls and insulation, natural gas fumes from ovens and heaters, and outgassing from plastics and synthetic fibers in clothes and furniture can plague a chemically sensitive child, leading to many of the same kinds of symptoms and problems described in the food allergies section of this chapter. Clinical ecologists can test the influence of these factors by eliminating each potentially offending substance from the environment, and then systematically reintroducing it while looking for changes in behavior or learning performance.

You may find that you need to create a "chemically-free oasis" for an especially sensitive child, setting up a bedroom or study room atmosphere that has hardwood floors or cotton scatter rugs instead of synthetic carpets, unvarnished wood furniture, and natural fabric clothes, pillows, and mattresses. You may also want to introduce an air purifier into your child's principal place of study, especially if there is a smoker in the house or you live in an area near heavy traffic or industrial pollution. The book *The Type 1/Type 2 Allergy Relief Program* by Alan Levin and Merla Zellerbach includes an excellent list of suppliers for nontoxic household items and environmental purifiers.

You have less control over air quality in your child's school but should be on the lookout for any obvious sources of pollutants. Check to see that the school has been examined for asbestos and make sure that the art supplies are safe. Recent legislation in California outlawed certain art materials because of their potentially harmful effects on students. Try to determine whether your child is allergic to chalk dust, ditto fluid, or other common educational nuisances. Some of these items can be checked by a clinical ecologist. While many of the above suggestions may seem unnecessary or impractical, "clearing the air" could represent one solid way that you can improve your child's learning climate.

Other ecological influences in learning include stress, expectation, and social-interaction—factors taken up in earlier chapters. Still other influences remain to be discussed, including temperature and such technological stressors as television, computers and video games. Your own approach to your child's eco-education will depend upon the unique factors of your environment. Putting together a positive program of environmental change may represent only a small contribution to the ecological problems of the world, but it could make a big difference to your child's learning life, transforming a turned-off or failing student into a happy learner. Isn't it worth a try?

The Learner of the Future

All education springs from some image of the future. If the image of the future held by a society is grossly inaccurate, its education system will betray its youth.

—Alvin Toffler

*O*ur public schools still look to the past for solutions to their educational dilemmas. Locked within an archaic structure, they struggle to make learning relevant to today's youth by leaning on past achievements, yet discover to their dismay that millions of youngsters have already moved into the future and left them far behind. The emergence of a new kind of learner is taking place across the country today, and the schools appear to be all but blind to this plain fact. Rather than taking the time to discover something about the phenomenon, the schools choose instead to label millions of these youngsters as disabled learners and ignore the learning potential in millions of others.

Two decades ago Marshall McLuhan pointed out that our culture had moved from a linear, print-oriented mode of learning to an electronic, space-age style where information is available instantaneously to everyone. The schools still operate according to the old orientation, while the child has moved swiftly into the new. McLuhan wrote, "Today's television child is attuned to up-to-the-minute 'adult' news—inflation, rioting, war, taxes, crime, bathing beauties—and is bewildered when he enters the nineteenth-century environment that still characterizes the educational establishment where information is scarce but ordered and structured by fragmented, classified patterns, subjects and schedules." McLuhan wrote this twenty years ago, but except for the addition of computers in education, his words still ring true in tens of thousands of classrooms across the country. Trapped in an obsolete setting, many children simply tune out.

Today's kids appear to be processing information in a very different way than yesterday's children. Perhaps as a way of coming to grips with the sheer volume of information that enters their lives every day, they've rejected the linear, classifying, and categorizing methods of parents and teachers—and embrace instead a learning style based on quick, multisensory scanning strategies. Tony Schwartz, author of *The Responsive Chord,* observed, "The educator would like his students to understand fully something they see or hear, and not miss any information. In an age of information overload, this is a death warrant. The student must learn to scan to live." And many students do scan in the classroom. They scan the walls, the ceiling, their peers, their imagination—anything but the lesson at hand.

It's almost ironic that the youngsters who appear to be most suited to the new demands of information overload could well be the so-called learning disabled. "Dyslexics are the wave of the future," proclaims Charles Drake, headmaster of the Landmark School in Prides Crossing, Massachusetts. Drake points out that as the requirements of society become increasingly complex, "the world's going to demand people who see relationships and who have problem-solving potential." We saw in the first chapter of this book how many so-called learning disabled kids possess superior creative and visualization abilities. Norman Geschwind wrote: "There have been in recent years an increasing number of studies that have pointed out that many dyslexics have superior talents in certain areas of non-verbal skill, such as art, architecture, engineering, and athletics." Other studies suggest that many of these kids process information holistically. They see the complete picture rather than the separate parts.

These global abilities are sorely needed in today's society.

It's said that there are 500,000 scientists worldwide working on weapons production. These scientists possess well-articulated and highly developed skills. They are products of some of the finest schools. However, even as they work intently on the technical requirements of their craft, they appear to be oblivious to the deeper consequences of their collective actions—the potential destruction of the planet. They see the parts but not the entire picture.

With so many other problems besetting humankind—pollution, racism, poverty, disease, and overpopulation among the most pressing—we need citizens who have vision, integrity, intuition, flexibility, creativity, and wisdom—not simply people who are good with numbers, words, and logic. Tragically, the schools may be writing off many children as school failures, underachievers, or disabled learners who possess these badly needed qualities. These youngsters may be the people Jonas Salk called the "evolvers" of the society, the change-agents who do things in a different way—their own way—and as a result, transform culture.

It's not surprising to look into the past and discover that many of the people who changed the way we live suffered from *schoolitis*. Albert Einstein didn't read until he was eight or nine and Woodrow Wilson, until he was nearly eleven. Thomas Edison once said: "I remember I used never to be able to get along at school. . . . I almost decided that I was a dunce." Teachers described Auguste Rodin, the sculptor, as "the worst pupil in school." Friedrich Nietzsche's parents thought he was retarded. Giacomo Puccini, the opera composer, consistently failed examinations. Teachers criticized Marcel Proust for writing disorganized compositions. Amy Lowell, the poet, was an atrocious speller. A thirteen year old tried unsuccessfully to teach Ludwig van Beethoven basic arithmetic. Many other great people, transplanted into contemporary society, would also probably have ended up in remedial or learning disability classes, including Winston Churchill, Pablo Picasso, Sergei Rachmaninoff, Leonardo da

Vinci, Henry Ford, William Butler Yeats, Agatha Christie, Hans Christian Andersen, and Gamal Abdel Nasser. Each of these talented people possessed an ability—scientific, artistic, musical, political, literary—that was irrelevant or even bothersome in a school setting but vital to the betterment of civilization.

In the same way, many children in our culture have abilities that put them at a disadvantage in the classroom but may be just what we need if our planet is to survive. I'm not just talking here about the gifted, the dyslexic, or the learning disabled, but ultimately about each and every child who has something to contribute to society—if only someone would recognize their ability and help them develop it. With schools focusing most of their attention on the good test-taker, the expert fill-in-the-blanker, and the hand-raiser who always has the "right answer," we're left with a situation in which 99.9 percent of the country's natural human resources could go undeveloped. A greater national tragedy could scarcely be envisioned.

But now you know that there are many ways of developing children's potential in and outside of the classroom. You should have a sound grasp of the range of their abilities based on Howard Gardner's theory of multiple intelligences, and a good, practical sense of how those abilities can be cultivated. You know now that these abilities can't be forced or speeded up, but they can be gently guided and nurtured. You should have a greater appreciation for the influence of "ecology" in children's lives, and realize that your own expectations can have a tremendous impact—for good or ill —on their learning potential. You know that you have several options for schooling children. Finally, you've seen—in spite of the gross malpractice of many public and private schools—the existence of numerous positive efforts among parents and teachers across the country to improve the conditions for learning among our children.

The Resources section that follows provides a wealth of materials that will help you implement some of this book's suggestions. Using these resources, you can construct inviting programs for children that draw on the spectrum of learning abilities—linguistic, logical-mathematical, spatial, bodily-kinesthetic, musical, interpersonal, and intrapersonal. By creating an environment tailor-made to their needs, you will help them really begin to learn—perhaps for the first time—in their own way.

Resources

How to Use This Section: The books, cassettes, journals, and organizations listed here are organized according to Gardner's seven types of intelligence, and by the following major categories: developmental issues; ecological issues; relaxation, stress, and learning; superlearning approaches; perspectives on learning styles; options in educating children; and books for children. Many of the books referred to in the text of *In Their Own Way* can be found here. Several of the books listed are not easily available in bookstores or libraries but can be ordered through the publisher. To find the addresses of publishers in this country, go to your public library and ask for *Books in Print, Vol. 7, Publishers* (New York: R.R. Bowker). You can order books directly or have a local bookstore do this for you. All the books listed are in print as of 1987. Several of the organizations listed below will send catalogs, pamphlets, brochures, or other materials for little or no cost.

LINGUISTIC INTELLIGENCE

Publications

ASHTON-WARNER, SYLVIA. *Teacher.* New York: Simon & Schuster, 1986. The "organic method" for teaching reading using a child's oral language.

BETTELHEIM, BRUNO, AND ZELAN, KAREN. *On Learning to Read: The Child's Fascination with Meaning.* New York: Knopf, 1982.

GROSS, JACQUELYN, AND GROSS, LEONARD. *Make Your Child a Lifelong Reader.* Los Angeles: Jeremy P. Tarcher, 1986.

KOCH, KENNETH. *Wishes, Lies and Dreams: Teaching Children To Write Poetry.* New York: Harper & Row, 1980.

MCGUIRE, JACK. *Creative Storytelling: Choosing, Inventing and Sharing Tales for Children.* New York: McGraw-Hill, 1985.

MOFFETT, JAMES. *A Student-Centered Language Arts Curriculum: Grades K–13.* 3d ed. Boston: Houghton Mifflin, 1983.

RICO, GABRIELLE LUSSER. *Writing the Natural Way.* Los Angeles: Jeremy P. Tarcher, 1983.

SMITH, FRANK. *Insult to Intelligence.* New York: Arbor House, 1986.

TRELEASE, JIM. *The Read Aloud Handbook.* Harmondsworth, England: Penguin, 1982. Suggests that reading is learned in the lap of a trusted adult.

ZAVATSKY, BILL, AND PADGETT, RON. eds. *The Whole Word Catalogue 2.* New York: McGraw-Hill, 1977.

Organizations

American Speech and Hearing Association, 10801 Rockville Pike, Rockville, MD 20852. Write for information on qualified audiologists in your area.

Educational Record Center, 472 East Paces Ferry Rd., Atlanta GA 30305. Tapes and records of classic children's and adult literature.

International Reading Association, Dept. TE, Box 8139, Newark, DE 19714.

National Association for the Preservation and Perpetuation of Storytelling, P.O. Box 309, Jonesborough, TN 37659.

National Council of Teachers of English, 1111 Kenyon Road, Urbana, IL 61801.

National Writing Project, 5635 Tolman Hall, University of California, Berkeley, CA 94720.

Teachers and Writers Collaborative, 5 Union Square W., New York, NY 10003. Many fine publications on reading and writing activities for children developed by teachers and writers working together.

LOGICAL-MATHEMATICAL INTELLIGENCE

Publications

BURNS, MARILYN. *The Book of Think: Or How to Solve a Problem Twice Your Size.* Boston: Little, Brown & Co., 1976.

BURNS, MARILYN. *The I Hate Mathematics Book.* Boston: Little, Brown & Co., 1975.

FURTH, HANS, AND WACHS, HARRY. *Thinking Goes to School.* New York: Oxford Univ. Press, 1974.

JACOBS, HAROLD. *Mathematics: A Human Endeavor.* San Francisco: W.H. Freeman, 1982. Grades 9–12.

KOHL, HERBERT. *Math, Writing and Games in the Open Classroom.* New York: Random House, 1974.

LORTON, MARY BARATTA. *Mathematics Their Way.* Menlo Park, CA: Addison-Wesley, 1976.

OVERHOLT, JAMES L. *Dr. Jim's Elementary Math Prescriptions.* Glenview, IL: Scott Foresman, 1978.

Parent-Teacher's Microcomputing Sourcebook for Children. New York: R.R. Bowker, 1985.

SAUL, WENDY, with NEWMAN, ALAN R. *Science Fare: An Illustrated Guide and Catalog of Toys, Books, and Activities for Kids.* New York: Harper & Row, 1986.

Organizations

Creative Publications, 5005 W. 110th Street, Oak Lawn, IL 60453. Innovative math materials.

Cuisenaire Co. of America Inc., 12 Church Street, New Rochelle, NY 10805.

Edmund Scientific, 101 E. Gloucester Pike, Barrington, NJ 07410. Science kits.

National Council of Teachers of Mathematics, 1906 Association Drive, Reston, VA 22091.

National Science Teachers Association, 1742 Connecticut Avenue N.W., Washington, DC 20009.

The Nature Company, P.O. Box 2310, Berkeley, CA 94702. High-quality science and nature study materials.

Science Curriculum Improvement Study, Delta Education, Box M, Nashua, NH 03061.

Young Scientists of America Foundation, P.O. Box 9066, Phoenix, AZ 85068. Association of science clubs.

SPATIAL INTELLIGENCE

Publications

DeMille, Richard. *Put Your Mother on the Ceiling: Children's Imagination Games.* Santa Barbara, CA: Santa Barbara Press, 1981.

Eberle, Robert F. *Scamper: Games for Imagination Development.* Buffalo, NY: DOK Publishers, 1971.

Edwards, Betty. *Drawing on the Right Side of the Brain.* Los Angeles: Jeremy P. Tarcher, 1979.

Fugitt, Eva. *He Hit Me Back First! Creative Visualization Activities for Parenting and Teaching.* Rolling Hills Estates, CA: Jalmar, 1982.

Gattegno, Caleb. *Words in Color.* New York: Educational Solutions, 1977.

Herzog, Stephanie. *Joy in the Classroom.* Boulder Creek, CA: Univ. of the Trees Press, 1982.

Huxley, Aldous. *The Art of Seeing.* Berkeley, CA: Creative Arts Books, 1982.

Kavner, Richard S. *Your Child's Vision.* New York: Simon & Schuster, 1985.

McKim, Robert H. *Experiences in Visual Thinking.* Monterey, CA: Brooks Cole, 1980.

Samples, Robert. *The Metaphoric Mind.* Reading, MA: Addison-Wesley, 1976.

Samuels, Mike, and Samuels, Nancy. *Seeing with the Mind's Eye: The History, Techniques and Uses of Visualization.* New York: Random House/Bookworks, 1975.

Shorr, Joseph E. *Go See the Movies in Your Head.* Santa Barbara, CA: Ross-Erickson, 1985.

Silberstein-Storfer, Muriel, and Jones, Mablen. *Doing Art Together.* New York: Simon & Schuster, 1982.

Singer, Jerome L., and Switzer, Ellen. *Mind-Play: The Creative Uses of Fantasy.* Englewood Cliffs, NJ: Prentice-Hall, 1980.

Woodcock, Richard W., Clark, Charlotte R., and Davies, Cornelia Oakes. *Peabody Rebus Reading Program.* Circle Pines, MN: American Guidance Service, 1979.

Cassettes

Ahsen, Akhter. *Imagery in the Classroom: Issues and Perspectives.* ProHelios, 397 N. Broadway, Suite 1–0, Yonkers, NY 10701.

Campbell, Gabe. *Education and Imagination.* (2-cassette set). Item No. 2520. A.R.E. Press, P.O. Box 595, Virginia Beach, VA 23451.

Organizations

American Optometric Association, 700 Chippewa Street, St. Louis, MO 63119.

National Art Education Association, 1916 Association Drive, Reston, VA 22091.

Optometric Extension Program, 2912 S. Daimler, Santa Ana,

CA 92705. Can provide referrals for behavioral optometrists in your area.

BODILY-KINESTHETIC INTELLIGENCE

Publications

CARR, RACHEL. *Be a Frog, a Bird or a Tree: Creative Yoga Exercises for Children.* New York: Harper & Row, 1977.

COBB, VICKI. *Science Experiments You Can Eat.* Philadelphia: Lippincott, 1972.

FELDENKRAIS, MOSHE. *Awareness through Movement.* New York: Harper & Row, 1972.

GELB, MICHAEL. *Body Learning: An Introduction to the Alexander Technique.* New York: Delilah Books, 1981.

GILBERT, ANNE G. *Teaching the 3 R's through Movement Experiences.* Edina, MN: Burgess International, 1977 (available through Macmillan).

MASTERS, ROBERT, AND HOUSTON, JEAN. *Listening to the Body: The Psychophysical Way to Health and Awareness.* New York: Delta, 1977.

METTLER, BARBARA. *Materials of Dance as a Creative Art Activity.* Tucson, AZ: Mettler Studios, 1979.

New Games Foundation. ANDREW FLUEGELMAN, ED. *The New Games Book.* Garden City, NY: Dolphin/Doubleday, 1976.

SCHNEIDER, TOM. *Everybody's a Winner: A Kid's Guide to New Sports and Fitness.* Boston: Little, Brown & Co., 1976.

SPOLIN, VIOLA. *Theater Games for the Classroom.* Evanston, IL: Northwestern Univ. Press, 1986.

STRIKER, SUSAN. *Please Touch.* New York: Simon & Schuster, 1986.

WEINSTEIN, MATT, AND GOODMAN, JOEL. *Playfair.* San Luis Obispo, CA: Impact, 1980.

WITKIN, KATE, AND PHILP, RICHARD. *To Move, to Learn.* New York: Schocken, 1978.

Organizations

American Alliance for Health, Physical Education, Recreation and Dance, 1900 Association Drive, Reston, VA 22091.

Child Life Play Specialities, Inc., P.O. Box 527, Holliston, MA 01746.

Community Playthings, Rifton, NY 12471.

Educational Teaching Aids, 199 W. Carpenter Avenue, Wheeling, IL 60090.

Edu-Kinesthetics, Inc., P.O. Box 5002, Glendale, CA 91201. Kinesiology ("touch for health") applied to education.

Lefthanders International, P.O. Box 8249, Topeka, KS 66608.

MUSICAL INTELLIGENCE

Publications

CAMPBELL, DON G. *Introduction to the Musical Brain.* St. Louis, MO: MMB Music, Inc., 1983.

HALPERN, STEVEN, AND SAVARY, LOUIS. *Sound Health: The Music and Sounds that Make Us Whole.* San Francisco: Harper & Row, 1985.

LINGERMAN, HAL A. *The Healing Energies of Music.* Wheaton, IL: Quest Books, 1983.

SUZUKI, SHINICHI. *Nurtured By Love: New Approach to Education.* Pompano Beach, FL: Exposition Press of Florida, 1982. By the founder of the Suzuki method of musical instrument playing.

Organizations

American Orff-Schulwerk Association, Department of Music, Cleveland State University, Cleveland, OH 44115.

Children's Book and Music Center, 2500 Santa Monica Boulevard, Santa Monica, CA 90404. Children's records, cassettes, and musical instruments.

Music Educators' National Conference, 1902 Association Drive, Reston, VA 22091.

Organization of American Kodaly Educators, Music Department, University of Wisconsin, Whitewater, WI 53190.

Suzuki Association of the Americas, P.O. Box 354, Muscatino, IA 52761.

THE PERSONAL INTELLIGENCES

Publications

ARMSTRONG, THOMAS. *The Radiant Child.* Wheaton, IL: Quest, 1985. Explores "peak experiences" in the life of the child.

BERENDS, POLLY BERRIEN. *Whole Child/Whole Parent.* rev. ed. New York: Harper & Row, 1983.

BRIGGS, DOROTHY CORKILLE. *Your Child's Self-Esteem.* Garden City, NY: Doubleday, 1970.

CANFIELD, JACK AND WELLS, HAROLD C. *100 Ways to Enhance Self-Esteem in the Classroom.* Englewood Cliffs, NJ: Prentice-Hall, 1976.

CLARKE, JEAN ILLSLEY. *Self-Esteem: A Family Affair.* San Francisco: Winston-Seabury, 1980.

CLEMES, HARRIS, AND BEAN, REYNOLD. *Raising Children's Self-Esteem.* New York: Zebra, 1982.

DREIKURS, RUDOLF AND STOLZ, VICKI. *Children: The Challenge.* New York: E. P. Dutton, 1987.

ELKINS, DOV PERETZ. *Glad to Be Me: Building Self-Esteem in Yourself and Others.* Rochester, NY: Growth Assoc., 1985.

GINOTT, HAIM. *Between Parent and Child.* New York: Avon, 1969.

GLASSER, WILLIAM. *Schools without Failure.* New York: Harper & Row, 1975.

GORDON, THOMAS. *P.E.T.: Parent Effectiveness Training.* New York: New American Library, 1976.

HOLT, JOHN. *How Children Fail.* New York: Dell, 1982.

JAMES, MURIEL, AND JONGEWARD, DOROTHY. *Born to Win.* New York: New American Library, 1978.

OAKLANDER, VIOLET. *Windows to Our Children.* Moab, UT: Real People Press, 1978.

PECK, JUDITH. *Leap to the Sun: Learning Through Dynamic Play.* Englewood Cliffs, N.J.: Prentice-Hall, 1979.

ROGERS, CARL. *Freedom to Learn for the Eighties.* Columbus, OH: Charles E. Merrill, 1983.

SATIR, VIRGINIA. *Peoplemaking.* Palo Alto, CA: Science & Behavior Books, 1972.

SIMON, SIDNEY, HOWE, LELAND, AND KIRSCHENBAUM, HOWARD. *Values Clarification.* New York: Dodd, Mead, 1985.

WICKES, FRANCES. *The Inner World of Childhood.* London: Coventure, 1977. Applies Carl Jung's ideas to child development.

Organizations

Argus Communications, P.O. Box 6000, One DLM Park, Allen, TX 75002. Materials for enhancing self-esteem and interpersonal communication.

National Council for Self-Esteem, c/o Constance H. Dembrowsky, P.O. Box 5700, Lincoln, NE 68505.

Uniquity, 215 4th Street, P.O. Box 6, Galt, CA 95632. Tools and publications for child therapy.

Zephyr Press, 430 South Essex Lane, Tucson, AZ 85711.

DEVELOPMENTAL ISSUES

Publications

AMES, LOUISE B., AND CHASE, JOAN A. *Don't Push Your Pre-Schooler.* New York: Harper & Row, 1981.

DODSON, FITZHUGH. *How to Parent.* New York: Signet, 1971.

ELKIND, DAVID. *The Hurried Child: Growing Up Too Fast, Too Soon.* Reading, MA: Addison-Wesley, 1981.

ERIKSON, ERIK. *Childhood and Society.* New York: Norton, 1950. Includes Erikson's famous "Eight Ages" model of human development.

LESHAN, EDA. *The Conspiracy Against Childhood.* New York: Atheneum, 1967.

MILLER, ALICE. *The Drama of the Gifted Child.* New York: Basic Books, 1981.

MONTESSORI, MARIA. *The Secret of Childhood.* New York: Ballantine, 1981.

PEARCE, JOSEPH CHILTON. *Magical Child.* New York: E.P. Dutton, 1977.

PIAGET, JEAN, AND INHELDER, BÄRBEL. *The Psychology of the Child.* New York: Basic Books, 1969. Perhaps Piaget's clearest introduction to his child development model.

WINN, MARIE. *Children without Childhood.* New York: Pantheon, 1983.

Organizations

Association for Childhood Education International, 11141 Georgia Avenue, Suite 200, Wheaton, MD 20902.

National Association for the Education of Young Children, 1834 Connecticut Avenue N.W., Washington, DC 20009.

ECOLOGICAL ISSUES

Publications

BELL, IRIS R. *Clinical Ecology.* Bolinas, CA: Common Knowledge Press, 1982. Short, clearly written introduction to this new field.

BRINK, JAN, AND RAMM, MELINDA. *S.N.A.C.K.S: Speedy, Nutritious, and Cheap Kids' Snacks.* New York: Signet, 1986.

BROD, CRAIG. *Techno-Stress: The Human Cost of the Computer Revolution.* Reading, MA: Addison-Wesley, 1984. Includes chapters on potential problems with children using computers.

COTT, ALAN. *Dr. Cott's Help for Your Learning Disabled Child: The Orthomolecular Treatment.* New York: Time Books, 1985.

CROOK, WILLIAM G. *Tracking Down Hidden Food Allergy.* Jackson, TN: Professional Books, 1980.

DADD, DEBRA LYNN. *The Nontoxic Home.* Los Angeles: Jeremy P. Tarcher, 1986. Excellent survey of potential toxic substances around the home and what to do about them.

FEINGOLD, BEN. *Why Your Child Is Hyperactive.* New York: Random House, 1985.

FERBER, RICHARD. *Solve Your Child's Sleep Problems.* New York: Simon & Schuster, 1985.

LAPPÉ, FRANCES MOORE. *What to Do after You Turn Off the TV.* New York: Ballantine, 1985.

LEVIN, ALAN SCOTT, AND ZELLERBACH, MERLA. *The Type 1/Type 2 Allergy Relief Program.* Los Angeles: Jeremy P. Tarcher, 1983.

MANDER, JERRY. *Four Arguments for the Elimination of Television.* New York: Morrow, 1978.

OTT, JOHN N. *Light, Radiation and You: How to Stay Healthy.* Greenwich, CT: Devin-Adair, 1985. Explores the impact of fluorescent lighting on learning.

SMITH, LENDON. *Feed Your Kids Right.* New York: Dell, 1982. Includes many recipes.

SMITH, LENDON. *Improving Your Child's Behavior Chemistry.* rev. ed. Englewood Cliffs, NJ: Prentice-Hall, 1984.

STEVENS, LAURA J., AND STONER, ROSEMARY B. *How to Improve Your Child's Behavior through Diet.* New York: Signet, 1981. Lots of recipes.

SUNSET MAGAZINE EDITORS. *Things You Can Make for Children.* Menlo Park, CA: Lane Publishing Company, 1986. Ideas for creating furniture and bedroom and play spaces.

VON HILSHEIMER, GEORGE. *How to Live with Your Special Child.* Washington, DC: Acropolis, 1970. One of the first books to emphasize ecological factors in learning.

WINN, MARIE. *The Plug-In Drug.* New York: Viking, 1985. Probes the negative effects of television viewing.

WUNDERLICH, RAY, AND KALITA, DWIGHT. *Nourishing Your Child.* New Canaan, CT: Keats, 1984.

Organizations

Society for Clinical Ecology, 2005 Franklin Street, Suite 490, Denver, CO 80205. Write them for information on a clinical ecologist in your area.

Duro-Lite Lamps Inc., 17–10 Willow Street, Fair Lawn, NJ 07410. Suppliers of Vita-Lite full-spectrum fluorescent lighting.

Feingold Association of the United States, P.O. Box 6550, Alexandria, VA 22306.

Human Ecology Action League (HEAL), P.O. Box 1369, Evanston, IL 60204.

RELAXATION, STRESS, AND LEARNING

Publications

ARENT, RUTH. *Stress and Your Child.* Englewood Cliffs, NJ: Prentice-Hall, 1984.

CURRAN, DOLORES. *Stress and the Healthy Family.* San Francisco: Winston-Seabury, 1985.

DOYLE, PATRICIA, AND BEHRENS, DAVID. *The Child in Crisis.* New York: McGraw-Hill, 1986.

FASSLER, JOAN. *Helping Children Cope: Mastering Stress through Books and Stories.* New York: Free Press, 1978.

HENDRICKS, GAY, AND ROBERTS, THOMAS. *The Second Centering Book: More Awareness Activities for Children, Parents and Teachers.* Englewood Cliffs, NJ: Prentice-Hall, 1977.

HUTH, HOLLY YOUNG. *Centerplay: Focusing Your Child's Energy.* New York: Simon & Schuster, 1984.

KERSEY, KATHERINE. *Helping Your Child Handle Stress.* Washington, DC: Acropolis, 1985.

KUCZEN, BARBARA. *Childhood Stress.* New York: Delacorte Press, 1982.

PROCACCINI, JOSEPH, AND KIEFABER, MARK W. *Parent Burnout.* New York: Signet, 1983.

RICHARDS, MARY. *I Am a Happy Learner . . . I am 100% OK.* Children's I AM Series, no. 74. Master Your Mind Tapes, 881 Hawthorne Drive, Walnut Creek, CA 94596 (cassette).

ROZMAN, DEBORAH. *Meditating with Children.* Boulder Creek, CA: Univ. of the Trees, 1975.

SAUNDERS, ANTOINETTE, AND REMSBERG, BONNIE. *The Stress-Proof Child.* New York: Signet, 1986.

YOUNGS, BETTIE B. *Stress in Children.* New York: Avon, 1985.

Organizations

The American Institute of Stress, 124 Park Avenue, Yonkers, NY 10703.

Parental Stress Inc., 654 Beacon Street, Boston, MA 02215.

SUPERLEARNING APPROACHES

Publications

BANDLER, RICHARD. *Using Your Brain—For a Change: Neurolinguistic Programming.* Moab, UT: Real People Press, 1985.

BUZAN, TONY. *Use Both Sides of Your Brain.* New York: E.P. Dutton, 1983.

CASEBEER, BEVERLY. *Using the Right/Left Brain: An Auditory Imagery Program.* Novato, CA: Academic Therapy, 1982.

CASTILLO, GLORIA. *Left-Handed Teaching.* New York: Holt, 1978.

DENNISON, PAUL E. *Switching On: The Holistic Answer to Dyslexia.* Glendale, CA: Edu-Kinesthetics Inc., 1981.

DILTS, ROBERT. *Applications of NLP.* Cupertino, CA: Meta Publications, 1983. Includes strategies for teaching spelling and other academic skills.

HARPER, LINDA. *Classroom Magic: Effective Teaching Made Easy.* Troy, MI: Twiggs Communications, 1982. Neurolinguistic programming techniques.

HELD, DEAN F. *The Intuitive Approach to Reading and Learning Disabilities.* Springfield, IL: Charles C. Thomas, 1984.

HOUSTON, JEAN. *The Possible Human.* Los Angeles: Jeremy P. Tarcher, 1982.

JACOBSEN, SID. *Meta-Cation: Prescriptions for Some Ailing Educational Processes.* Cupertino, CA: Meta Publications, 1983. A personal account of the use of neurolinguistic programming in education.

LOZANOV, GEORGI. *Suggestology and Outlines of Suggestopedy.* New York: Gordon & Breach, 1978.

OSTRANDER, SHEILA, AND SCHROEDER, LYNNE. *Superlearning.* New York: Delta, 1986.

PRICHARD, ALLYN, AND TAYLOR, JEAN. *Accelerating Learning: The Use of Suggestion in the Classroom.* Novato, CA: Academic Therapy, 1980.

The VAK International NLP Newsletter, 1433 Webster Street, Palo Alto, CA 93401. Quarterly. Information about new developments in neurolinguistic programming and education.

VITALE, BARBARA MEISTER. *Unicorns Are Real: A Right-Brained Approach to Learning.* New York: Warner, 1985.

WILLIAMS, LINDA VERLEE. *Teaching for the Two-Sided Mind.* New York: Simon & Schuster, 1986.

Organizations

Barzak Educational Institute, 6 Knoll Lane, Suite A2, Mill Valley, CA 94941.

Learning in New Dimensions, P.O. Box 14487, San Francisco, CA 94114. Workshops in suggestopedia, holistic education, and neurolinguistic programming techniques. Sells super-learning tapes.

New Learning Pathways, 6000 E. Evans, Bldg. 2, #250, Denver, CO 80222. Neurolinguistic programming applied to learning problems.

The Society for Accelerative Learning and Teaching Inc., Box 1216, Welch Station, Ames, IA 50010. Major center for superlearning in the United States. Publishes journal.

SES Associates, 121 Brattle Street, Cambridge, MA 02138. Developers of synectics, a method of creativity development.

PERSPECTIVES ON
LEARNING STYLES

Publications

ALVINO, JAMES. *Parents' Guide to Raising a Gifted Child: Recognizing and Developing Your Child's Potential.* Boston: Little, Brown & Co., 1985.

Academic Therapy, 20 Commercial Boulevard, Novato, CA 94947. Professional journal published five times a year with many practical methods for working with learning-different children.

Brain-Mind Bulletin, P.O. Box 42211, Los Angeles, CA 90042. Newsletter published every three weeks. Frequent articles on new approaches to learning.

COLES, GERALD S. The Learning Mystique: A Critical Look at Learning Disabilities. New York: Pantheon, 1987.

DIXON, JOHN PHILO. *The Spatial Child.* Springfield, IL: Charles C. Thomas, 1983.

DUNN, RITA, AND DUNN, KENNETH. *Teaching Students through Their Individual Learning Styles.* Reston, VA: Reston Publishing Co., 1978.

FADELY, JACK L., AND HOSLER, VIRGINIA N. *Understanding the Alpha Child at Home and School.* Springfield, IL: Charles C. Thomas, 1979. Argues that many children labeled learning disabled need to be recognized as "alpha children" with a different but not necessarily disabled pattern of neurological organization.

FLEMING, ELIZABETH. *Believe the Heart: Our Dyslexic Days.* San Francisco: Strawberry Hill Press, 1984. Dyslexia needs to be recognized as a hidden strength.

GARDNER, HOWARD. *Frames of Mind.* New York: Basic Books, 1983. Presents Gardner's theory of seven intelligences.

Gifted Child Monthly, Box 115, Sewell, NJ 08080.

Gifted Child Today, P.O. Box 637, 100 Pine Avenue, Holmes, PA 19043.

Journal of Learning Disabilities, 5341 Industrial Oaks Boulevard, Austin, TX 78735.

LAWRENCE, GORDON. *People Types and Tiger Stripes: A Practical Guide to Learning Styles.* Gainesville, FL: Center for Applications of Psychological Type, 1984. Focuses on Carl Jung's theory of psychological types.

LYNN, ROA. *Learning Disabilities: An Overview of Theories, Approaches, and Politics.* New York: Free Press, 1979.

McGUINESS, DIANE. *When Children Don't Learn.* New York: Basic Books, 1985. Discusses important learning differences between males and females.

Ross, ALAN O. *Learning Disability: The Unrealized Potential.* New York: McGraw-Hill, 1980.

SIMPSON, EILEEN. *Reversals: A Personal Account of Victory over Dyslexia.* New York: Washington Square, 1979.

Organizations

American Association for Gifted Children, 15 Gramercy Park, New York, NY 10003.

Council for Exceptional Children, 1920 Association Drive, Reston, VA 22091.

Creative Education Foundation, 437 Franklin Street, Buffalo, NY 14202.

Foundation for Mind Research, Box 600, Pomona, NY 10970. Jean Houston, director. Workshops in human potential.

Latebloomers Educational Consulting Services, P.O. Box 5435, Santa Rosa, CA 95402. Thomas Armstrong, founder. Individual work with children and adults. Workshops for parent and teacher organizations.

Learning Styles Network, St. John's University, Grand Central and Utopia Parkways, Jamaica, NY 11430.

National Association for Children and Adults with Learning Disabilities, 4156 Library Road, Pittsburgh, PA 15234.

National Association for Gifted Children, 5100 N. Edgewood Drive, St. Paul, MN 55112. Publishes *Gifted Child Quarterly.*

National Foundation for Gifted and Creative Children, 395 Diamond Hill Road, Warwick, RI 02886.

National Learning Laboratory, 8417 Bradley Boulevard, Bethesda, MD 20817. Dedicated to raising and expanding intelligence.

New Horizons for Learning, P. O. Box 51140, Seattle, WA 98115–1140. An international network that disseminates the latest research in learning styles, new approaches to education, and more.

Orton Dyslexia Society, 724 York Road, Baltimore, MD 21204.

OPTIONS IN EDUCATING CHILDREN

Publications

ANDERSON, WINIFRED, CHITWOOD, STEPHEN, AND HAYDEN, DEIDRE. *Negotiating the Special Education Maze.* Englewood Cliffs, NJ: Prentice-Hall, 1982. Practical advice for parents on using special education laws to benefit children.

BROWN, MARTHA. *Schoolwise: A Parent's Guide to Getting the Best Education for Your Child.* Los Angeles: Jeremy P. Tarcher, 1985.

COLLINS, MARVA. *Marva's Way.* Los Angeles: Jeremy P. Tarcher, 1982. A Chicago school principal's prescriptions for success.

FRITH, TERRY. *Secrets Parents Should Know about Public Schools.* New York: Simon & Schuster, 1985.

GRANGER, BILL, AND GRANGER, LORI. *The Magic Feather: The Truth about Special Education.* New York: E. P. Dutton, 1986.

HOLT, JOHN. *Teach Your Own.* New York: Delacorte/Seymour Lawrence, 1981. Discusses schooling your child at home.

KOHL, HERBERT. *Thirty-Six Children.* New York: Signet, 1973. Alternative education in a large urban public school.

LONG, KATE. *Johnny's Such a Bright Boy, What a Shame He's Retarded.* Boston: Houghton Mifflin, 1977. A plea in favor of mainstreaming (placing special needs children into regular classrooms).

Learning 87, P.O. Box 2580, Boulder, CO 80322. Innovative teaching ideas for elementary grades. Teacher focus but can be applied to teaching your child at home.

Mothering, P.O. Box 8410, Santa Fe, NM 87504. Quarterly magazine. Focus on birthing and parenting issues, but includes regular section on alternative educational approaches.

NEILL, A. S. *Summerhill.* New York: Pocket, 1984.

NEMKO, MARTY, AND NEMKO, BARBARA. *How to Get Your Child a "Private School" Education in a Public School.* Washington, DC: Acropolis, 1986.

Parenting, 501 2nd Street, San Francisco, CA 94007.

Parents Magazine, P.O. Box 3055, Harlan, IA 51593. Monthly.

PRIDE, MARY. *The Big Book of Home Learning.* Westchester, IL: Good News Pub. Available from Good News Pub., 9825 W. Roosevelt Road, Westchester, IL 60153.

RICHARDS, MARY CAROLINE. *Towards Wholeness: Rudolf Steiner Education in America.* Middletown, CT: Wesleyan Univ. Press, 1980. Includes a listing of Waldorf Schools in the United States.

Roeper Review, Roeper City and County School, P.O. Box 329, Bloomfield Hills, MI 48013. Gifted education.

Organizations

American Montessori Society, 150 Fifth Avenue, New York, NY 10011.

Growing Without Schooling, 729 Boylston Street, Boston, MA 02116. Network of parents who are teaching children at home. Newsletter and mail order service.

Hewitt Research Foundation, P.O. Box 9, Washougal, WA 98671. Home schooling advocates. Christian focus.

National Association for the Legal Support of Alternative Schools, Box 2823, Santa Fe, NM 87501.

National Coalition for Alternative Community Schools, 1289 Jewett Street, Ann Arbor, MI 48104.

National Parent Teacher Association (PTA), 700 N. Rush Street, Chicago, IL 60611.

Networking Institute, 296 Newton Street, Suite 350, Waltham, MA 02154. Will help you network with other parents who share your perspectives on learning and education.

Nienhuis-Montessori USA, 320 Pioneer Way, Mountain View, CA 94040. Suppliers of Montessori material.

North American Montessori Teacher's Association, 2859 Scarborough Road, Cleveland Heights, OH 44118. Publishes directory of Montessori schools nationwide.

North Dakota Study Group on Evaluation, Center for Teaching and Learning, University of North Dakota, Grand Forks, ND 58201. Alternative methods for evaluation of children's academic progress.

BOOKS FOR CHILDREN

GILBERT, SARA. *Using Your Head: The Many Ways of Being Smart.* New York: Macmillan, 1984. Excellent guide to the different kinds of "smart" including body smart, book smart, people smart and art smart (gr. 5–9).

KETTELKAMP, LARRY. *Your Marvelous Mind.* Philadelphia, PA: Westminster Press, 1980. Superlearning techniques for kids including activities to improve memory, visualization, and imagination (gr. 5–8).

KRAUS, ROBERT. *Leo the Latebloomer.* New York: Windmill, 1971. A wonderful tale about patience and growth (preschool and up).

PRESTON, EDNA. *The Temper Tantrum Book.* Harmondsworth, England: Penguin, 1976 (preschool–3).

MACDONALD, SUSE. *Alphabatics.* New York: Bradbury Press, 1986.

MAYER, MERCER. *There's a Nightmare in my Closet.* New York: Dial, 1968. (gr. K–3.)

SENDAK, MAURICE. *Where the Wild Things Are.* New York: Harper & Row, 1963. (gr. K–3.)

SILVERSTEIN, SHEL. *A Light in the Attic.* New York: Harper & Row, 1981. (gr. 4–6.)

SIMON, NORMA. *I Was So Mad!* Niles, Il: A. Whitman, 1974. (gr. K–2.)

SIMON, NORMA. *Why Am I Different?* Chicago: Albert Whitman and Co., 1976. A celebration of learning differences (gr. K–3).

VIORST, JUDITH. *Alexander and the Terrible Horrible No Good Very Bad Day.* New York: Atheneum, 1977. (gr. K–4.)

Notes

Notes are referenced by chapter, page, and the first few words of the sentence to which the note refers.

Chapter 1: The Worksheet Wasteland

p. 1. "Billy shut . . ." Jean Houston, *The Possible Human* (Los Angeles: Jeremy P. Tarcher, 1982), 137.

p. 2. "Susan wrote . . ." Charles Meisgeier, Constance Meisgeier, and Dorothy Werblo, "Factors Compounding the Handicapping of Some Gifted Children," *Gifted Children Quarterly* (Fall 1978): 329.

p. 2. "All three of these boys . . ." Susan Baum, "Meeting the Needs of Learning Disabled Gifted Students," *Roeper Review* (September 1984).

p. 3. "Einstein once wrote . . ." Quoted in Victor Goertzel and Mildred G. Goertzel, *Cradles of Eminence* (Boston: Little, Brown and Co., 1962), 253.

p. 4. "Less than 3 percent . . ." John Goodlad, *A Place Called School* (New York: McGraw-Hill, 1984), 229–230.

p. 4. "When students were asked . . ." Goodlad, 234.

p. 4. "Goodlad comments: . . ." Goodlad, 223.

p. 5. "Nationally, sales of . . ." Quoted in George Madaus, *Phi Delta Kappan* (May 1985):616.

p. 5. "A study conducted by . . ." National Commission on Excellence in Education, *A Nation at Risk* (Washington, DC: U.S. Dept. of Education, 1983), 21.

p. 5. "And a recent report . . ." "Becoming a Nation of Readers: A Commission's Recommendations," *Education Digest* (October 1985):13.

p. 5. "During the past 15 years . . ." Goodlad, 105.

p. 6. "Goodlad points out . . ." Goodlad, 109.

p. 7. "He suggested that they . . ." Samuel Kirk, "Learning Disabilities: A Historical Note," *Academic Therapy* 17, no. 1 (September 1981):7.

p. 7. "Bob Algozzine, a professor . . ." James Tucker, Linda J. Stevens, and James E. Ysseldyke, "Learning Disabilities: The Experts Speak Out," *Journal of Learning Disabilities* 16, no. 1 (January 1983):9.

p. 7. "It seems such a shame . . ." Douglas Friedrich, Gerald B.

Fuller, and Donald Davis, "Learning Disability: Fact and Fiction," *Journal of Learning Disabilities* 17, no. 4 (April 1984):209.

p. 8.　"The horrifying truth is . . ." Mary Poplin, "Summary Rationalizations, Apologies and Farewell: What We Don't Know about the Learning Disabled," *Learning Disability Quarterly* 7 (Spring 1984):133.

p. 8.　"She speculated that . . ." Sara G. Tarver, Patricia S. Ellsworth, and David J. Rounds, "Figural and Verbal Creativity in Learning Disabled and Nondisabled Children," *Learning Disability Quarterly* 3 (Summer 1980):11–18.

p. 9.　"Other authorities affirm . . ." Norman Geschwind, "Why Orton Was Right," *Annals of Dyslexia* 32 (1982):22.

p. 9.　"Jean Symmes, a psychologist . . ." Jean S. Symmes and Judith L. Rappaport, "Unexpected Reading Failure," *American Journal of Orthopsychiatry* 42 (1972):82–91.

p. 9.　"And Dorothy Bullock . . ." Dorothy Bullock and Salvatore Severe, "Using Fantasy and Guided Visual Imagery," *Academic Therapy* 16 (January 1981):311–316.

p. 11.　"Their new life in . . ." Quoted in Ernest Schactel, *Metamorphosis* (New York: Basic Books, 1959), 293.

p. 12.　"In spite of this . . ." Roger Lewin, "Is Your Brain Really Necessary?" *Science* 210 (December 12, 1980):1232–1234.

p. 12.　"The 1,000 classrooms . . ." Goodlad, 105.

Chapter 2: Seven Ways to Bloom

p. 16.　"They appear to involve . . ." See Howard Gardner, *Frames of Mind: The Theory of Multiple Intelligences* (New York: Basic Books, 1983), 84–91, 118–120, 156–159, 181–184, 210–213, 260–267, for a more complete description of the neurological basis for the seven intelligences.

p. 17.　"So he began singing . . ." Mel Tillis and Walter Wager, *Stutterin' Boy* (New York: Dell, 1986), 77.

p. 17.　"By the age . . ." Gardner, 110.

p. 17.　"Sixty percent of . . ." Gardner, 202.

p. 17.　"In certain South Sea . . ." Gardner, 338–341.

p. 17.　"Finally, many non-Western . . ." Gardner, 272.

p. 18.　"We happen to live . . ." Quoted in J. E. Bogen, "Some Educational Aspects of Hemispheric Specialization," *Dromenon* 1, no. 5–6 (February 1979):18–19.

p. 25.　"Gardner cautions . . ." Gardner, 386–87.

Chapter 3: Testing for Failure

p. 26.　"Twenty years ago . . ." Banesh Hoffmann, *The Tyranny of Testing* (New York: Crowell-Collier, 1962).

p. 27.　"The National Education Association . . ." *National Education*

Association Handbook, 1984–85 (Washington, DC: National Education Association of the United States, 1984), 240.

p. 27.   "This test is supposed . . ." Cited in Jerome Sattler, *Assessment of Children's Intelligences and Special Abilities* (Boston: Allyn & Bacon, 1982), 160.

p. 28.   "According to Harvard professor . . ." Steven Jay Gould, *The Mismeasure of Man* (New York: W.W. Norton, 1981).

p. 28.   "And as David Owen . . ." David Owen, *None of the Above: Behind the Myth of Scholastic Aptitude* (Boston: Houghton Mifflin Co., 1985).

p. 29.   "We don't know what . . ." Gerald S. Coles, "The Learning Disability Test Battery: Empirical and Social Issues," *Harvard Educational Review* 48 (1978):313–340.

p. 29.   "A New York teacher . . ." Pat Carini, *The School Lives of Seven Children: A Five Year Study* (Grand Forks, ND: North Dakota Study Group on Evaluation, 1982), 39.

p. 30.   "This testing room . . ." Thomas A. Sebeok and Robert Rosenthal, eds., *The Clever Hans Phenomenon: Communication with Horses, Whales, Apes and People* (New York: New York Academy of Sciences, 1981).

p. 31.   "As San Diego State . . ." Hugh Mehan, Alma Hertweck, and J. Lee Meihls, *Handicapping the Handicapped: Decision Making in Students' Educational Careers* (Stanford, CA: Stanford Univ. Press, 1986), 100.

p. 39.   "George Madaus, director . . ." George Madaus, "Test Scores as Administrative Mechanisms in Educational Policy," *Phi Delta Kappan* (May 1985):616.

Chapter 4: Dysteachia

p. 42.   "Whether they actually . . ." P. Kenneth Komoski, "What Do We Need to Improve Instructional Materials?" *Education Digest* (October 1985):15.

p. 43.   "Anne Adams of . . ." Quoted in Craig Pearson, "Reading vs. Reading Skills," *Learning* (November 1980): 29.

p. 44.   "Research suggests . . ." Jeannine Oakes, *Keeping Track: How Schools Structure Inequality* (New Haven, CT: Yale Univ. Press, 1985).

p. 45.   "As a result . . ." U.S. Dept. of Commerce, *Statistical Abstract of the United States* (Washington, DC: U.S. Government Printing Office, 1984).

p. 45.   "Today these activities . . ." Kenneth Kavale and P. Dennis Matson, "One Jumped Off the Balance Beam: Meta-Analysis of Perceptual-Motor Training," *Journal of Learning Disabilities* 16, no. 3 (March 1983).

p. 45.   "However, when one . . ." Norman Silberberg and Margaret

Silberberg, "Myths in Remedial Education," *Journal of Learning Disabilities* 2, no. 4 (April 1969).

p. 45. "Carl Milofsky, a California . . ." Carl Milofsky, *Special Education: A Sociological Study of California Programs* (New York: Praeger, 1976), 106.

p. 46. "Lee Ann Trusdell . . ." "How Pull-Out Programs Can Hurt," *Learning* (March 1980):17.

p. 46. "Jeanne Westin interviewed . . ." Jeanne Westin, "Educationally Handicapped: The Social Engineers' Gold Mine?" in *The Coming Parent Revolution* (New York: Rand McNally, 1981), 132.

p. 46. "As a federal study . . ." Nicholas Hobbs, *The Futures of Children: Categories, Labels and Their Consequences* (San Francisco: Jossey-Bass, 1975), 81.

p. 48. "The rats in the . . ." Mark R. Rosenzweig, Edward L. Bennett, and Marian Cleeves Diamond, "Brain Changes in Response to Experience," *Scientific American* 226 (February 1972):22–29.

p. 52. "In their classic book . . ." Peter Schrag and Diane Divoky, *The Myth of the Hyperactive Child* (New York: Pantheon, 1975).

Chapter 5: Learning in Their Own Way

p. 60. "Now thirty years . . ." Rudolf Flesch, *Why Johnny Can't Read* (New York: Harper & Row, 1986).

p. 70. "This fair included . . ." Linda Robertson, "A Celebration of Learning," *Principal* (November 1985):28–31.

p. 70. "Suggest that they . . ." See Roger Williams, "Why Children Should Draw," *Saturday Review* (September 3, 1977).

Chapter 6: Bodywise

p. 73. "Albert Einstein, . . ." Quoted in Richard L. Masland, "The Advantages of Being Dyslexic," *Bulletin of the Orton Society* 26 (1976):16.

p. 73. "William James, . . ." William James, *Principles of Psychology* (New York: Henry Holt, 1910), 2:61.

p. 74. "When *legere* and *lectio* . . ." Quoted in Marshall McLuhan, *The Gutenberg Galaxy* (Toronto, Canada: Univ. of Toronto Press, 1965), 89.

p. 75. "Yet medical doctors . . ." For a sound debunking of the neurological hypothesis for learning disabilities, see Gerald Coles, *The Learning Mystique: A Critical Look at Learning Disabilities* (New York: Pantheon, 1987).

p. 76. "Michael Gelb . . ." "Gelb: Freeing the Body to Free the Mind for Learning," *Brain-Mind Bulletin* (January 2, 1984):2.

p. 78. "She timed his oral . . ." Betty Brenneman, "A Field Report: Putting the Body Back into the Learning Equation," *Somatics* (Spring/Summer 1985):14.

p. 82. "Her braille teacher . . ." Lois E. McCoy, "Braille: A Language for Severe Dyslexics," *Journal of Learning Disabilities* 8, no. 5 (May 1975):34.

p. 82. "One study observed . . ." Cited in McCoy, p. 33 (see above).

p. 83. "Even kids who read . . ." For more information on obtaining materials that teach braille, write the National Braille Association, 1290 University Avenue, Rochester, NY 14607. For information on sign language, see Cindy Cochran, *Signing with Cindy* (Houston: Gulf Pub. Co., 1982).

Chapter 7: The Inner Blackboard

p. 86. "Jerome Bruner, . . ." Jerome Bruner, Rose R. Olver, and Patricia M. Greenfield, *Studies in Cognitive Growth* (New York: Wiley, 1966).

p. 86. "George Lakoff . . ." George Lakoff and Mark Johnson, *Metaphors We Live By* (Chicago: Univ. of Chicago Press, 1980).

p. 86. "Titchner came to associate . . ." Rudolf Arnheim, *Visual Thinking* (Berkeley, CA: Univ. of California Press, 1969), 111.

p. 87. "Eugene S. Ferguson . . ." Eugene S. Ferguson, "The Mind's Eye: Nonverbal Thought in Technology," *Science* 197 (August 26, 1977):827–836.

p. 89. "Research suggests that . . ." Amiram Carmon, Israel Nachshon, and Ruth Starinsky, "Developmental Aspects of Visual Hemifield Differences in Perception of Verbal Material," *Brain and Language* 3 (1976):463–469.

p. 90. "During the course . . ." Barbara Cordoni, "Teaching the LD Child to Read through Visual Imagery," *Academic Therapy* 16, no. 3 (January 1981):327–331.

p. 90. "With two basic . . ." Kiyoshi Makita, "The Rarity of Reading Disability in Japanese Children," *American Journal of Orthopsychiatry* 38 (1968):599–614.

p. 90. "They wrote: . . ." Paul Rozin, Susan Poritsky, and Raina Sotsky, "American Children with Reading Problems Can Easily Learn to Read English Represented by Chinese Characters," *Science* 171 (March 26, 1971): 1264–1267.

p. 93. " 'But if you make . . .' " A. C. Harwood, *The Recovery of Man in Childhood* (London: Hodder & Stoughton, 1958), 79–80.

p. 93.   "In teaching about . . ." W. J. J. Gordon and Tony Poze, *Strange and Familiar* (Cambridge, MA: Synectics Education Systems, 1972).

p. 94.   "Studies indicate that . . ." Ralph Norman Haber, "Eidetic Images," *Scientific American* (April 1969).

p. 94.   "E. R. Jaensch, . . ." E. R. Jaensch, *Eidetic Imagery* (New York: Harcourt, Brace & Co., 1930).

p. 94.   "One junior high . . ." Penny Righthand, "Kids Master Spelling by Using Personal Viewing Screens," *San Francisco Examiner,* March 14, 1984.

Chapter 8: Teaching with Feeling

p. 101. "We have been brought up . . ." Quoted in Constance Holden, "Paul MacLean and the Triune Brain," *Science* 204 (June 8, 1979):1068.

p. 101. "He calls these codes . . ." "New Theory: Feelings Code, Organize Thinking," *Brain-Mind Bulletin* 7, no. 6 (March 8, 1982).

p. 101. "Some researchers go . . ." "Heart, brain may be partners," *Brain-Mind Bulletin* 12, no. 6 (March 2, 1987).

p. 101. "Finally, Jerome Bruner, . . ." Jerome Bruner, *Actual Minds, Possible Worlds* (Cambridge, MA: Harvard Univ. Press, 1986), 69.

p. 101. "Lesley Hart, an educator . . ." Lesley Hart, "Misconceptions about Learning Disabilities," *The National Elementary Principal* 56, no. 1 (September/October 1976).

p. 102. "Yet, I'm reminded . . ." John Goodlad, *A Place Called School* (New York: McGraw-Hill, 1984), 108.

p. 103. "Several ways of releasing . . ." See John L. Carter and Harold L. Russell, "Use of EMG Biofeedback Procedures with Learning Disabled Children in a Clinical and an Educational Setting," *Journal of Learning Disabilities* 18, no. 4 (April 1985):213–216; J. T. Hopkins and L. J. Hopkins, "A Study of Yoga and Concentration," *Academic Therapy* 14, no. 3 (1979):314–345; and E. Rivera and M. M. Omizo, "An Investigation of the Effects of Relaxation Training on Attention to Task and Impulsivity Among Male Hyperactive Children," *The Exceptional Child* 27, no. 1 (1980):41–51.

Chapter 9: The Learning Network

p. 119. "I noticed recently . . ." Quoted in *Growing without Schooling Newsletter* 18 (1977):3.

p. 122. "Nineteenth-century British . . ." Erica Carle, "Children as Teachers," in *Human Learning* (American Society of Humanistic Education, 1970).

Chapter 10: Great Expectations

p. 125. "He hypothesized, . . ." Robert Rosenthal and Lenore Jacobsen, *Pygmalion in the Classroom: Teacher Expectations and Pupils' Intellectual Development* (New York: Holt, 1968).

p. 125. "The group informed . . ." Glen G. Foster, Carl R. Schmidt, and David Sabatino, "Teacher Expectancies and the Label Learning Disabilities," *Journal of Learning Disabilities* 9 (1976):58–61.

p. 125. "Another study showed . . ." R. Parker, S. Larsen, and T. Roberts, "Teacher-Child Interactions of First-Grade Students Who Have Learning Problems," *The Elementary School Journal* 81 (1981):163–171.

p. 126. "It's no wonder . . ." G. Bingham, "Self-Esteem among Boys with and without Specific Learning Disabilities," *Child Study Journal* 10 (1980):41–47.

p. 126. "Psychologists are now . . ." Lynn Grimes, "Learned Helplessness and Attribution Theory: Redefining Children's Learning Problems," *Learning Disability Quarterly* 4 (Winter 1981):91–100.

p. 131. "He never drew . . ." Stanley Krippner, "The Ten Commandments that Block Creativity," *Gifted Child Quarterly* (Autumn 1967):144–156.

p. 132. "She suggests that . . ." Diane McGuinness, *When Children Don't Learn: Understanding the Biology and Psychology of Learning Disabilities* (New York: Basic Books, 1985).

Chapter 11: A Patient Attitude

p. 134. "TEACHER: 'Monitors are you . . .'" Jules Henry, "A Cross-Cultural Outline of Education," *On Education* (New York: Random House, 1971), 150.

p. 134. "Thirty years ago, . . ." Henry, 151.

p. 135. "A joint statement . . ." Barbara Vobejda, "Preschools Accused of Pushing Tots Too Hard," *The Washington Post*, November 15, 1986:A1,18.

p. 136. "Anthropologist Edward T. Hall . . ." Edward T. Hall, *The Hidden Dimension* (New York: Doubleday, 1969), 132.

p. 136. "Such countries as . . ." John Downing, "How Society Creates Reading Disability," *The Elementary School Journal* 77, no. 4 (March 1977).

p. 137. "Dr. Louise Bates Ames, . . ." Louise Bates Ames, "Learning Disabilities Often Result from Sheer Immaturity," *Journal of Learning Disabilities* 1, no. 3 (March 1968):207–212.

p. 137. "Citing the work . . ." Raymond S. Moore and Dorothy N. Moore, *Better Late than Early* (New York: Reader's Digest Press, 1977).

p. 138. "He emphasized that . . ." Eleanor Duckworth, "Either We're Too Early and They Can't Learn It or We're Too Late and They Know It Already: The Dilemma of Applying Piaget," *Harvard Educational Review* 49, no. 3 (August 1979):297–312.

p. 138. "Steiner observed: . . ." Rudolf Steiner, *The Kingdom of Childhood* (London: Rudolf Steiner Press, 1964), 40.

p. 139. "Here, for example, . . ." A. S. Neill, *Summerhill* (New York: Hart, 1960), 30.

p. 140. "To parents who . . ." Hazrat Inayat Khan, *The Sufi Message* 2 (The Netherlands: Servire Wassenaar, 1976):173.

p. 141. "He had just turned . . ." Louise Bates Ames, "Learning Disability—Very Big around Here," *Research Communications in Psychology, Psychiatry and Behavior* 10, nos. 1 & 2 (1985):26.

p. 141. "The nonreader may . . ." Norman E. Silberberg and Margaret C. Silberberg, "The Bookless Curriculum: An Educational Alternative," *Journal of Learning Disabilities* 2, no. 6 (June 1969):302–307.

p. 141. "Adolescents could perhaps . . ." Desson Howe, "Reaching the Stars: VIPs Who Overcame Dyslexia Honored," *The Washington Post,* October 31, 1985, B12.

p. 142. "Anthropologist Ashley Montagu . . ." Ashley Montagu, *Growing Young* (New York: McGraw-Hill, 1983).

p. 143. "In *The Hurried Child,* . . ." David Elkind, *The Hurried Child* (Reading, MA: Addison-Wesley, 1981), 177–178.

p. 143. "Earl Ogletree, a Chicago . . ." Earl J. Ogletree, "Intellectual Growth in Children: The Theory of 'Bioplasmic Forces,'" *Phi Delta Kappan* (February 1974):407–412.

Chapter 12: The Doors of Perception

p. 146. "Heinz Werner, one of . . ." Heinz Werner, *Comparative Psychology of Mental Development* (New York: International Universities Press, 1973), 88.

p. 146. "He offers examples . . ." Werner, 89.

p. 146. "This mixing of . . ." Werner, 90.

p. 146. "He wrote . . ." Werner, 69.

p. 146. "He illustrated this . . ." Werner, 73.

p. 146. "A four-year-old . . ." Werner, 74.

p. 148. "This idea became . . ." R. L. Gregory, *Eye and Brain: The Psychology of Seeing* (New York: McGraw-Hill, 1973), 216–17.

p. 149. "Ray Gottlieb, a California . . ." "School Anxiety May Be Major Cause of Myopia," *Brain-Mind Bulletin* 7, no. 17 (October 25, 1982).

p. 149. "Helmer Myklebust, a well-known . . ." Helmer Myklebust, *Auditory Disorders in Children: A Manual for Differential Diagnosis* (New York: Grune & Stratton, 1954).

p. 150. "Tim Gallwey, author . . ." "How-To Instructions Inhibit Optimum Performance," *Brain-Mind Bulletin* 7, no. 13 (August 2, 1982).

p. 151. "Maureen Murdock, a California . . ." Maureen Murdock, *Spinning Inward* (Culver City, CA: Peace Press, 1982), 48.

p. 152. "An Alabama mother . . ." *Growing without Schooling Newsletter* (1981) 18:11.

p. 152. "Holt commented: . . ." John Holt, *Teach Your Own* (New York: Delta/Seymour Lawrence, 1981), 239.

Chapter 13: The Ecology of Learning

p. 160. "Dr. Hugh Powers, a Texas . . ." Hugh Powers, *Food Power: Nutrition and Your Child's Behavior* (New York: St. Martin's Press, 1978).

p. 160. "As Carole S. Weinstein . . ." Carole S. Weinstein, "The Physical Environment of the School," *Review of Educational Research* 49, no. 4 (1979):585.

p. 162. "The new field of . . ." " 'Chronopsychology' Links Brain Function to Cycles," *Brain-Mind Bulletin* 7, no. 1 (November 23, 1981).

p. 163. "After forty minutes . . ." Tony Buzan, *Use Both Sides of Your Brain* (New York: E.P. Dutton, 1974), 50.

p. 163. "Dr. Sheldon Cohen . . ." S. Cohen, G. W. Evans, D. S. Krantz, D. Stokols, and S. Kelly, "Aircraft Noise and Children: Longitudinal and Cross-Sectional Evidence on Adaptation to Noise and the Effectiveness of Noise Abatement," *Journal of Personality and Social Psychology* 40 (1981):331–345.

p. 164. "One study equipped . . ." Lewis W. Mayron, "Ecological Factors in Learning Disabilities," *Journal of Learning Disabilities* 11, no. 8 (October 1978):44.

p. 165. "One study reported . . ." Cited in Esther R. Sinofsky and Frederick G. Knirk, "Choose the Right Color for Your Learning Style," *Instructional Innovator* (March 1981):17.

p. 166. "Yet a recent study . . ." Charles Moon, Mike Marlowe, John Stellech, and John Errera, "Main and Interaction Effects of Metallic Pollutants on Cognitive Functioning," *Journal of Learning Disabilities* 18, no. 4 (April 1985):217–221.

p. 167. "Recent legislation in . . ." *Not a Pretty Picture: Art Hazards in California Public Schools* (Berkeley: California Public Interest Research Group, August 1984).

Afterword: The Learner of the Future

p. 169. " 'All education springs . . .' " Alvin Toffler, ed., *Learning for Tomorrow: The Role of the Future in Education* (New York: Random House, 1974), 3.

p. 169. "McLuhan wrote, . . ." Marshall McLuhan and Quentin Fiore, *The Medium Is the Massage* (New York: Bantam, 1967), 18.

p. 170. "Tony Schwartz, author . . ." Tony Schwartz, *The Responsive Chord* (Garden City, NY: Anchor Press/Doubleday, 1973), 113.

p. 170. "Drake points out . . ." Quoted in Roa Lynn, *Learning Disabilities: An Overview of Theories, Approaches, and Politics* (New York: The Free Press, 1979), 19–20.

p. 170. "Norman Geschwind wrote: . . ." Norman Geschwind, "Why Orton Was Right," *Annals of Dyslexia* 32 (1982):22.

p. 170. "Other studies suggest . . ." See, for example, John R. Kershner, "Rotation of Mental Images and Asymmetries in Word Recognition in Disabled Readers," *Canadian Journal of Psychology* 33, no. 1 (1979):39–49; and Sandra Witelson, "Developmental Dyslexia: Two Right Hemispheres and None Left," *Science* 195 (January 21, 1977):309–311.

p. 171. "Many other great people . . ." See Victor Goertzel and Mildred G. Goertzel, *Cradles of Eminence* (Boston: Little, Brown & Co., 1962); Lloyd Thompson, "Language Disabilities in Men of Eminence," *Bulletin of the Orton Society* 19 (1969); Jan Ehrenwald, *Anatomy of Genius* (New York: Human Sciences Press, 1984); and R. S. Illingworth and C. M. Illingworth, *Lessons From Childhood* (London: Livingstone, 1966).

Index

positive side of, 8–9, 13, 18, 88–90, 170–172
self-concept and, 125–126
stress and, 98, 101–102, 137
symptoms of (reframed), 127–128
Learning disabilities movement and special education, 44–46
history of, 6–8
tests used in, 28–30
Learning Disability Quarterly, 8
Learning ecology, 156–167
Lefthandedness, 75, 152
Light (as an ecological factor in learning), 164–165
Linguistic intelligence, 14–16, 19–20, 57, 61, 64, 67
Logical-mathematical intelligence, 14–16, 20–21, 57, 62, 64, 67–68
Lowell, Amy, 171
Lozanov, Georgi, 77

McLuhan, Marshall, 169
Mainstreaming, 46
Mathematics, 63–66, 80–81, 91–92
Meditation. *See* Relaxation
Memory, 36, 94
Menuhin, Yehudi, 129
Metaphor, 93
Miller, Alice, 133
Minimal brain damage, 12, 18, 75
Model schools, 70
Montessori, Maria, 52–53, 163
Motivation, 56–57
Multiplication, 63–66, 91–92
Multisensory learning, 151
Musical intelligence, 15–17, 22, 58, 62, 65–68
Myopia, 149

Nash, Ogden, 155
Nasser, Gamal Abdel, 172
National Education Association, 26–27
Neill, A.S., 139
Neurolinguistic programming, 94

Neurological development. *See* Brain functioning
Neurological dysfunction, 75
Nietzsche, Friedrich, 171
Normality, 132
Nutrition. *See* Diet

Optometrists, 153
Oral language, 61, 74–75. *See also* Storytelling
Organic reading, 109–110
Orthomolecular medicine, 159

Parent-child relationships, 106–107, 113–123
Parent cooperative schools, 53
Parents
  as facilitators, 106–107, 114–123
  as models, 118–120
  as school volunteers, 51, 70
Parent-teacher relationships, 120–122
Paycheck, Johnny, 16
Peer teaching, 122–123
Perception, 145–150
  exercises in, 153–155
  See also Sensory experience
Personal intelligences. *See* Interpersonal intelligence; Intrapersonal intelligence
Phonics instruction, 60–61
Piaget, Jean, 47, 73, 137–138, 145, 152, 162
Picasso, Pablo, 171
Poetry writing, 109
Praise, 50, 116, 130–131
Proust, Marcel, 171
Psychoneurology. *See* Brain functioning
Puccini, Giacomo, 171
Punishment, 116
Pygmalion effect, 125

Rachmaninoff, Sergei, 171
Readiness programs, 134–135
Reading, 39, 42–43, 45, 60–63, 112, 119, 143